Contents

The first three chapters of this book have been excerpted from Pet Bassett Hound, by Mrs. Travis Look, © 1956 by All-Pet Books, Inc.

EDITED BY DIANE McCARTY

Photo credits: Vince Serbin: pp. 5, 6 (below), 8, 10, 11, 13, 14, 15, 16 (above), 17, 20, 22, 25, 26, 30, 32, 33, 37, 38, 39, 40, 42, 46 (above), 48, 114 (above), 115, 118, 119, 121, 122, 123, 125; Fritz Prenzel: p. 7; Anne Roslin Williams: p. 116; Evelyn M. Shafer: p. 46 (below); Louise Van der Meid: 16 (below). Mr. Serbin's photos made possible through the cooperation of: Gwen McCullagh, Brendan's Bassets, Skillman, NJ; and Mrs. Betty Henderson, Henderson's Basset Kennels, Little Silver, NJ. Tracking photos depict Am., Can. Ch. Brendan's Bellroute Squire, Am., Can. Companion Dog.

ISBN 0-87666-679-9

© 1979 by T.F.H. Publications, Inc.

Distributed in the U.S. by T.F.H. Publications, Inc., 211 West Sylvania Avenue, P.O. Box 427, Neptune, N.J. 07753; in England by T.F.H. (Gt. Britain) Ltd., 13 Nutley Lane, Reigate, Surrey; in Canada to the book store and library trade by Beaverbooks, 953 Dillingham Road, Pickering, Ontario L1W 1Z7; in Canada to the pet trade by Rolf C. Hagen Ltd., 3225 Sartelon Street, Montreal 382, Quebec; in Southeast Asia by Y.W. Ong, 9 Lorong 36 Geylang, Singapore 14; in Australia and the South Pacific by Pet Imports Pty. Ltd., P.O. Box 149, Brookvale 2100, N.S.W., Australia; in South Africa by Valiant Publishers (Pty.) Ltd., P.O. Box 78236, Sandton City, 2146, South Africa; Published by T.F.H. Publications, Inc., Ltd., The British Crown Colony of Hong Kong. Printed in Hong Kong.

BASSET HOUNDS

1

2

6

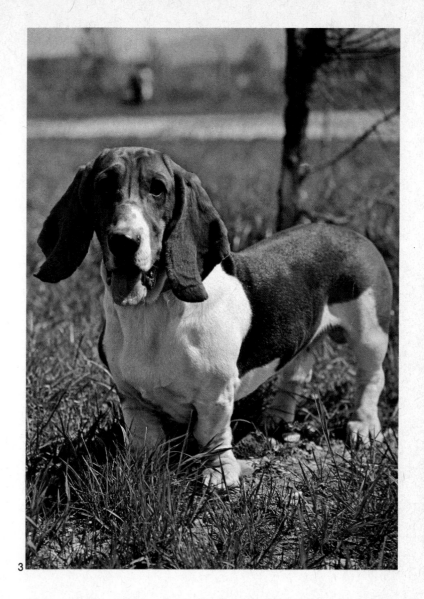

3

(1) A youngster enjoying the thrill of participating in an outdoor show with his Basset Hound. Photo courtesy of Robert M. Weiss, Edison, NJ. (2) A box full of Bassets! This young litter will remain together at least until they're weaned and ready to go to new homes. (3) A Basset in the field: a hearty specimen takes a break during an exercise outing. Bassets, like all dogs, will welcome the opportunity to exercise out of doors.

The Basset Hound, efficient in the field and docile in the home, is steadily growing in popularity.

1. ORIGINS

The Basset Hound, a sad-eyed, slow-moving dog, has maintained through the years a high level of popularity, due to its expertise in the hunt and its docility in the home. Whether the Basset Hound you buy is intended for field trialing or as a household pet, this is a breed not to be ignored. And, indeed, it *is not* ignored—according to American Kennel Club registrations, the Basset Hound's popularity is ever-increasing.

Serious huntsmen have long been aware of the merits of this most deliberate scent hound, who tracks his quarry with sureness, in his own way and in his own time. Whether he is tracking foxes, rabbits or pheasants, the Basset Hound can be depended upon to make his way easily through heavy ground cover, and giving plenty of "tongue" (sounding to alert the hunter).

If one member of the household is to train or hunt with the Basset, spending a good amount of time with him, an unbreakable bond will develop between the two, and no one else will garner the same enthusiastic response from the dog as his true "master." The Basset Hound is an exceptionally loyal dog, and while some may view his ways as being stubborn and sluggish, it may well be that he only reacts with a special vigor for his beloved master.

EUROPEAN ORIGINS

The St. Hubert hound was the forerunner of our Basset Hound and many other kinds of scent hounds which appear all over the world. The St. Hubert hound is reported to have been developed by the abbots of the monastery bearing that name and located in the French forest region of Ardennes. St. Hubert founded his order during the early years of the sixth century. Legend has it that before he became an abbot, St. Hubert was a happy-go-lucky, carefree young nobleman who loved to hunt, and who was miraculously converted one Sunday by seeing a vision of a deer with a cross between its horns.

With a deeply rooted love of the hunt, he set out to develop a new strain of hound dog in his kennel at the France-Belgium border and indeed the hounds of St. Hubert were of a very distinct type. All early accounts describe them as being black and tan with heavy heads, long ears, long bodies and comparatively short and heavy legs. There was also a longer-legged, white variety developed. Both types had wonderfully keen noses and deep melodious voices. The long ears of the breed assisted

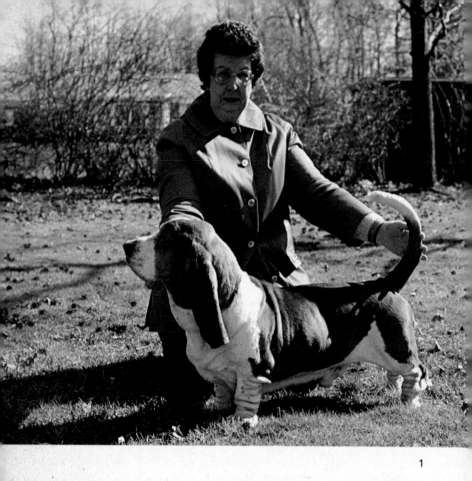

1

(1) Preparing your Basset Hound for an appearance before the judges in a show ring will include teaching the correct show stance. Here, this woman "stacks" her Basset in the proper pose. (2) Two young Bassets enoy an outing in a grassy field. Whenever possible, allow your pet to enjoy the healthful benefits of fresh air and sunshine. (3) A Basset Hound enjoying his favorite chew treat, a flavorful nylon bone. Such a bone offers excellent and safe chewing exercise.

2   3

A gathering of Basset Hounds awaits the call of the hunter. The call signals the start of a trek into the fields, in search of small game.

them, then as now, in their hunting by acting as a sort of "fan," blowing the scent up from the ground toward the dogs' noses. Of course, the original purpose of these hounds was somewhat different than it it today—the abbots who worked to create this breed used the longer-legged strains to hunt boar and wolves, and required a dog of incredible stamina and fearlessness. While these traits are still retained in the conscientiously-bred Basset Hounds, the game that is now pursued by the breed is of a less ferocious type—small woods animals such as raccoons and the like.

When St. Hubert bred *small* legged specimens to each other, it was because when the abbots hunted small game, the thick ground cover of the Ardennes required a hunting dog to keep his nose steadily to the ground. In longer legged dogs, this was a bit of a physical impossibility, as the dog's back and neck would no doubt begin to ache if he were stooped for long periods. Thus, as the legs of the Bassets got shorter, so too did they get more crooked, until they arrived at the seemingly gnarled, stumpy type we see today.

In temperament, the St. Hubert hounds were described as being mild, obedient and so gentle that they were not useful for killing game but only for trailing it. It is now believed that the Basset Hound as we know it today was developed over the years by careful selection and breeding of the short-legged specimens, and by the inclusion in the breeding program of "sports" or mutants, with very short legs. Many early accounts refer to

1

(1) The short legs that are prized in the Basset Hound are clearly evident in this illustration. (2) This Basset may appear sad-eyed, but he is obviously enjoying his favorite chew product, a ham-flavored nylon bone.

2

14

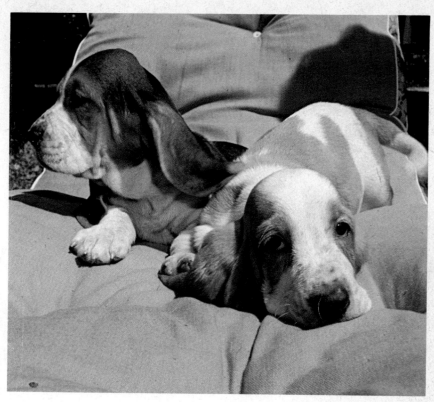

4

(1) A fine head study of a Basset, illustrating the pendulous ears and wrinkled facial skin. (2) A Basset pup having some fun in a new found "toy." (3) If your Basset won't be allowed on the furniture, train him early on to stay down on the floor, or else he will be a stubborn disciplinary problem later. (4) A charming pose: two sleepy Bassets enjoying the out of doors on a comfy chaise longue.

(1) An adorable Basset pup having some fun with a toy. (2) Bassets generally have even temperaments and will welcome some frisky play from the household cat. However, don't leave the dog alone with kittens lest he play too rough.

1

2

the Bloodhound and give rise to the idea that somewhere there was a cross between it and the Basset Hound. Authorities now agree that such was not actually the case, for in the early days a Bloodhound was a dog of any breed of known bloodlines whose breeding had been recorded.

As time passed, St. Hubert hounds became scattered over various parts of France and were crossed with local types until all colors were developed. The name "Basset," as derived from the French "bas," means "low set." It is reported by early authorities that the name was applied to any hound that stood under 16 inches high. France was indeed a land of many strains of hound, each developed to suit local hunting conditions. Most long-legged strains had their counterpart in the short-legged, or "basset" type. As with the dogs bred by the abbots of St. Hubert's monastery, the larger hounds were used by mounted hunters for hunting deer, boar, wolves and stag, while the short-legged variety was maintained for hunting smaller game afoot in heavier cover.

The Basset Hound of France was later to develop into three main types: the smooth-coated, the half-rough coated, and the rough-coated. Each of these types had their followers, who preferred the straight leg,

Despite their seeming slowness, Basset Hounds are quite alert, and will sound a resounding bark to alert you to the presence of a stranger on your property.

the slightly crooked leg, or the full crook. Thus, there were many types created over the centuries, reaching what was probably their peak of popularity during the 18th century.

By searching through English literature, one can find references to the St. Hubert hound or to hounds of this type which indicate that these dogs were imported into England as long ago as the 15th century. It is said that James IV of Scotland imported Bassets which were used to rout game, driving the animals into the open. The hunters would then release their swift gazehounds, who would run down and catch the quarry. Although this breed or type of hound was known in England over the years, it was never, to our knowledge, bred there until the end of the 19th century.

TWO PROMINENT FRENCH STRAINS

In France, Basset Hounds, for some unknown reason, lost much of their following during the early part of the 19th century, and it became increasingly difficult to find a good specimen or a true-breeding strain. The revival of interest in the breed was due to the work of two brilliant breeders, the Comte le Couteulx de Canteleu, and Monsieur Lane, who, working in the latter part of the century, were able to bring the breed back to a high order of quality. These gifted men worked with about the same stock, but each developed a different and distinct type of Basset Hound. The original Lane hound was pale tan and white, lemon and white, or badger pied. They had splendid earage, and were very large, heavy dogs with tremendously crooked forelegs—so much so that they tired rather quickly in the field. They had magnificent voices, but they lacked drive. However, once on the line they would stick to it with wonderful tenacity.

The strain developed by the Comte le Couteulx was smaller and livelier than that of Monsieur Lane and had straighter forelegs. These Bassets were black, white, and tan of a very rich color. Their heads were broader, ears higher-set and shorter, and the eyes were larger and more prominent. In the field they had more initiative, but lacked, perhaps, some of the tenacity of the Lane hounds and some of the quality of voice. These two families were eventually fused into one, which combined to a large extent the better qualities of both. This strain eventually became known as the Basset Artesian-Normand, or the Basset d'Artois; it is the direct forerunner of our present day Basset Hounds.

As the popularity of the breed continued to grow in France, the Artois became very common, and a second type, the Vendeen or Griffon (rough or wire coated) became, if anything, more popular. Today, visitors to France report more of the rough coated Bassets in evidence, especially at

18

A depiction of the Bassets Artesian-Normand, the direct forerunners of our our present-day Basset Hounds. The strain was developed by the merging of two strains, those of the Comte le Couteulx and of Monsieur Lane. Photo from *Hounds of the World,* by Sir William Buchanan Jardine.

shows, than the smooth coated type. Less well known but equally attractive were the Blue Gascon (blue mottled, or white with black spots of varying size, and tan marks above the eyes), and the Ardennes (black and tan or solid red), which existed prior to World War II in more quantity than they do today. Many times one finds throwbacks to these types in litters, even though many generations of Bassets intervene.

BASSETS ON THE BRITISH SHOW SCENE

The first Basset Hound to be exhibited at a dog show in England was imported in 1875 from France by Sir Everett Millais. Named "Model," he was a Basset d'Artois. Other breeders imported excellent specimens of the rough-coated type and it was this type which found for many years in the Royal Kennels and exhibited by the Prince of Wales.

In 1882, Lord Onslow sold an entire pack of Bassets to Sir Everett Millais and George Krehl. The pack consisted of 15 pairs of magnificent Bassets, from whom all the finest Basset Hounds in England and America are descended. It was Sir Everett who so aptly described these

(1) The Basset Hound is continually growing in popularity, with young healthy specimens like this being sought as pets and field companions. (2) A pair of snoozing Basset pups.

dogs as "small running hounds." With Krehl, Sir Everett did much to foster the breed's popularity in England.

THE BASSET HOUND IN AMERICA

The history of the Basset Hound in America takes the breed back to the days of the first American president. According to George Washington's voluminous diary, the first Basset Hounds were sent to America by Washington's friend, Lafayette, following the Revolution. This information throws light on the origin of the so-called "old Virginia bench-legged Beagle." Nothing is known about imports to America during the next hundred years, although undoubtedly Bassets were brought to the states as companions by the many newcomers arriving from foreign lands.

The American Kennel Club registered its first Basset Hound in 1885. The registration reads: "Bouncer, No. 3234, by Major x Venus. Owner, Collin Cameron, Brickerville, Pa. Breeder, Pottinger Dorsey, New Market, Va. Whelped March 1881, Black, tan and white."

In 1935, a group of Michigan breeders met at the Detroit dog show and formed the Basset Hound Club of America. In addition to those present, 12 prominent breeders from throughout the country were invited to become charter members. During the year 1937, the club members succeeded in qualifying as an AKC member club.

During the 1940's, purebred dogs of all breeds began to feel the influence of a steadily growing interest among the general public, and although World War II did much to dissipate this interest, it resumed in full force when hostilities ended in mid decade.

By 1950, a Basset Hound had become a world-famous television star, and "Mr. Morgan," as he was called, caused the breed to become quite popular. Indeed, interest in the breed has continued to grow, and the registrations listings put out by the American Kennel club attest to this. In 1930, the Basset occupied 50th place; in 1940, 38th place; 1956, 16th place; and, moving up to 1978, 23rd place.

Will this breed continue its upward surge and move into, say, the top 10 within the next dozen or so years? Only time will tell, but if the past is any indication, we can be assured that our beloved Basset Hound will become even more prominent on the show circuit, tracking fields, and, a spot he readily and lovingly occupies, in the family home.

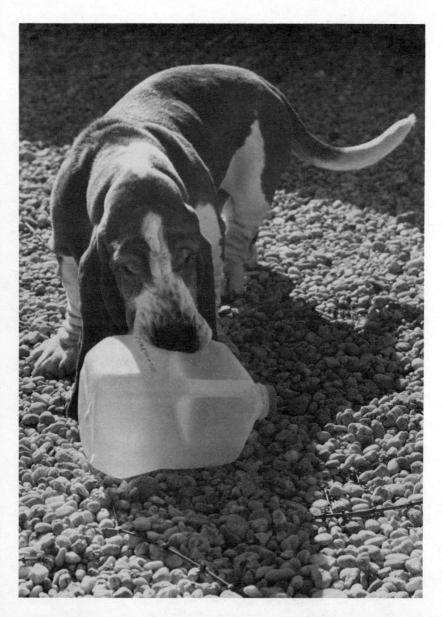

Bassets are known to perform amusing antics to delight onlookers—as is evidenced by this display! These dogs truly love attention—whether in the form of an "audience" or a doting family—so it is best to have a Basset only if you can give plenty of time to it.

2. DESCRIPTION AND STANDARD

Since his first introduction, the Basset Hound has progressed, but, although his head and expression are, as a rule, almost handsome, and perhaps more beautiful than are to be found on any other hound, his unduly long body and crooked legs are, as in the case of the Dachshund, likely to prevent his ever being a popular idol. Still, he has many admirers, for he is quiet, sensible and attractive . . . As a companion he is affectionate; and kept clean and nicely groomed, his expression and gaudy markings are sure to attract attention anywhere; and he is not so quarrelsome as our own hounds.

Rawdon B. Lee in *Modern Dogs,*
Vol. II
(Sporting Division) 1897

How true, as Rawdon wrote, that the Basset's head is outstanding, but how untrue that his form and that of the Dachshund would mitigate against their popularity, which for both breeds has climbed steadily in the past decade. Much of the charm and attractiveness of both breeds is precisely their comical appearance. In the case of the Basset Hound, the magnificent, perfectly-proportioned head contrasts so completely with the utterly out-of-proportion body and legs that the dog is indeed quaint and amusing. This contrast is enhanced by the typical expression of great dignity, intelligence and the sobriety expressed in the beautiful eyes, and also by the behavior of the Basset who knows that he is a clown. Bassets seem to set about deliberately to amuse their audience, and then after making everyone laugh, they look at you with that woebegone, reproachful stare. It is this quality that has had much to do with making this breed the perfect television dog, appearing on many programs as the family pet.

A CREATURE OF HABIT
The Basset Hound is a creature of habit and is readily trained because of it. He is truly a thoughtful and clever dog; you can explain what you want, demonstrate it to him, and in a few lessons the habit is set. He takes

great pleasure in his achievements and enjoys his lessons.

Not an active dog unless on a hunting trip, the Basset Hound makes an ideal house dog, for he is not one to jump on and off furniture, rush to the door when the bell rings, or to the windows whenever people pass by, and as a pup he is not especially destructive. The dog is content to stay near his family, sleeping on his own comfortable bed or the softest armchair if allowed. But when the children are home and want to play, the lazy Basset will come to life and join in willingly. It is next to impossible to annoy a Basset, so they can be depended upon to roughhouse and play with children of all ages. They make no enemies among other dogs, and their mildness enables them to live with any kind of pet in true harmony, even rabbits!

EXERCISE REQUIREMENTS

If ever there was an armchair athlete, it is the Basset Hound. On the other hand, if you give him a purpose out of doors such as a pleasant walk in the park or a day in the fields hunting rabbits and birds, your Basset will don his other personality and perform his part of the activity with tireless energy and enthusiasm. This ability to take what comes and enjoy it to the fullest makes the Basset able to live just about any place that any dog can live. They seem to thrive anywhere, and when kept in cold climates they develop a dense short coat. In warm climates their coat remains thin and comfortable all year 'round.

Your Basset Hound, if a house pet, requires a walk at least three times a day and whenever possible these walks should provide the dog with a chance to move along briskly. The length of time you walk him depends almost entirely on your own schedule and inclination. Suffice to say he should be allowed plenty of opportunity to relieve himself, and to enjoy his change of scenery.

Unless you live in the country, remote from busy highways and have a large expanse of land, it is not sensible to allow your dog, no matter what the breed, to run at large. Bassets, being a friendly breed, are easy to steal, easy to poison, and, (being slow) they have trouble successfully dodging automobiles. It is easy to see, therefore, why the city-kept Basset Hound should remain safely in the front yard or in the house until it is time to take him out on the leash. Your new Basset Hound will be a precious addition to your household, and as such you will want to ensure his safety.

For those of us who like to do a bit of hunting now and then, the Basset Hound makes a splendid companion. He will trail a rabbit, pheasant, or grouse for you in a very satisfactory manner, and he is a born woodsman, impossible to lose and as sure-footed as a fly.

Basset Hounds relish the opportunity to indulge in a pleasant walk in the park with their masters. One or two such leisurely walks a day should be enough to satisfy the exercise needs of this "armchair athlete."

SELECTING THE BEST BASSET HOUND

When you set out to buy your Basset puppy, it is well to be sure whether you are getting a dog to be a pet only, or one which you can, perhaps, show and use for breeding. The individual dogs should be clean and in good condition. Puppies that are in good health have shiny coats, bright eyes, are responsive when you speak to them, and they are plump (not just fat in the middle, with hip bones sticking up). Their bones should be heavy and their feet very large, compared with any other breed. The legs should be short. When moving about, a pup should track true. His hindquarters should be round, with no sign of weakness or bad coordination. If you are buying a show type pup, inspect its teeth to see that the bite is a correct scissors bite, eyes are (preferably) dark, ears thin and long and set as low as possible. The back should be without a roach; even as a young pup, a Basset should have a "prow," that is, the frontal bone of the chest sticks out. The rib cage should be smooth, long and nicely rounded. Avoid thin, splayed feet, as they never correct themselves, and are not desirable show-wise. Pick a pup whose skin hangs in folds.

A Basset pup at seven or eight weeks is heavy and fat with moderately good coordination. But until it is well grown, no Basset pup should be allowed or encouraged to jump on and off steps, porches, furniture or from heights of any sort. See to it that your new pup keeps all four feet on the ground as much as possible. The reason for this restriction is that the distorted joints of the Basset, combined with its unusual weight for its age, make a pup vulnerable to dislocations and wrenches. Many a promising show prospect has had his chances spoiled by receiving an injury of this type which rendered him lame or off-gaited for life.

Lifting a Basset pup must be done in a special way, due to his length and weight. Never under any circumstances lift or pull a puppy by his front legs; it is not only very painful to him but may result in dislocation. Use both hands to support the weight of your pup: one hand between the front legs and one hand under the hindquarters. Do not carry him by the middle, as this is very uncomfortable and puts a great strain on the pup.

If your pup was raised in a kennel, it is unlikely that he is familiar with ordinary house noises such as the clatter of pans, slamming of doors, and radio and television programs. Try to introduce these things to your Basset easily; show him they are harmless, and he will soon take them in stride. But it is asking a lot of an inexperienced pup to comprehend that

When selecting the Basset Hound puppy that will become the newest addition to your family, choose one that appears generally healthy and alert. If you have any doubts, have your veterinarian check the pup before you make a final purchase.

all these new and strange noises are just part of daily life.

Once you have your new puppy home, you will find that he wishes to be with you constantly. If you shut him in the kitchen, he will make mournful sounds and will persist with considerable tenacity. It is probably wisest to expect to spend the first three or four days and nights with your new Basset Hound pup. Once he is familiar with his new home and family he can be taught to stay where you want him to stay, when you want him to, although it means enduring some heart-rending wails a few times.

You will find that the average Basset Hound thinks as slowly as he moves. Do not rush at your new pup, shouting various commands. All that you'll achieve by doing this is to utterly confuse him, and he will simply go blank. It is easy to encourage and gently direct your pup to do anything you wish, and once he comprehends your orders, he'll be only too glad to follow them. A Basset is intensely devoted to its family and is very affectionate and intelligent. Praise and pats of approval are what they love most.

THE BASSET HOUND STANDARD

If, as mentioned earlier, you choose to buy a show prospect Basset Hound puppy, there are specifics that you should look for. Knowledge of the official standard by which the Basset Hound is judged in the show ring will be of great help in selecting the right pup.

The standard, as prescribed by the national breed club and approved by the American Kennel Club, sets the guidelines for the "ideal" dog. Breeders use the standard as a guide of perfection, exemplifying the type of dog for which to strive. Show judges use the standard to closely examine each entrant that comes before them in the ring, determining just how closely each dog comes to approaching the ideal for his particular breed.

STANDARD FOR THE BASSET HOUND

General Appearance: The Basset Hound possesses in marked degree those characteristics which equip it admirably to follow a trail over and through difficult terrain. It is a short-legged dog, heavier in bone, size considered, than any other breed of dog, and while its movement is deliberate, it is in no sense clumsy. In temperament it is mild, never sharp or timid. It is capable of great endurance in the field and is extreme in its devotion.

Head: The head is large and well proportioned. Its length from oc-

27

ciput to muzzle is greater than the width at the brow. In over-all appearance the head is of medium width. **The skull:** is well domed, showing a pronounced occipital protuberance. A broad flat skull is a fault. The length from nose to stop is approximately the length from stop to occiput. The sides are flat and free from cheek bumps. Viewed in profile the top lines of the muzzle and skull are straight and lie in parallel planes, with a moderately defined stop. The skin over the whole of the head is loose, falling in distinct wrinkles over the brow when the head is lowered. A dry head and tight skin are faults. **The muzzle** is deep, heavy, and free from snipiness. **The nose** is darkly pigmented, preferably black, with large wide-open nostrils. A deep liver-colored nose conforming to the coloring of the head is permissible but not desirable. **The teeth** are large, sound, and regular, meeting in either a scissors or an even bite. A bite either overshot or undershot is a serious fault. **The lips** are darkly pigmented and are pendulous, falling squarely in front and, toward the back, in loose hanging flews. **The dewlap** is very pronounced. **The neck** is powerful, of good length, and well arched. **The eyes** are soft, sad, and slightly sunken, showing a prominent haw, and in color are brown, dark brown preferred. A somewhat lighter-colored eye conforming to the general coloring of the dog is acceptable but not desirable. Very light or protruding eyes are faults. **The ears** are extremely long, low set, and when drawn forward, fold well over the ends of the nose. They are velvety in texture, hanging in loose folds with the ends curling slightly inward. They are set far back on the head at the base of the skull and, in repose, appear to be set on the neck. A high set or flat ear is a serious fault.

Forequarters: **The chest** is deep and full with prominent sternum showing clearly in front of the legs. **The shoulders** and elbows are set close against the sides of the chest. The distance from the deepest point of the chest to the ground, while it must be adquate to allow free movement when working in the field, is not to be more than one-third the total height at the withers of an adult Basset. The shoulders are well laid back and powerful. Steepness in shoulder, fiddle fronts, and elbows that are out, are serious faults. **The forelegs** are short, powerful, heavy in bone, with wrinkled skin. Knuckling over of the front legs is a disqualification. **The paw** is massive, very heavy with tough heavy pads, well rounded and with both feet inclined equally a trifle outward, balancing the width of the shoulders. Feet down at the pastern are a serious fault. **The toes** are neither pinched together nor splayed, with the weight of the forepart of the body borne evenly on each. The dewclaws may be removed.

Body: The rib structure is long, smooth, and extends well back. The ribs are well sprung, allowing adequate room for heart and lungs. Flatsidedness and flanged ribs are faults. The topline is straight, level, and free from any tendency to sag or roach, which are faults.

Hindquarters: The hindquarters are very full and well rounded, and are approximately equal to the shoulders in width. They must not appear slack or light in relation to the over-all depth of the body. The dog stands firmly on its hind legs showing a well-let-down stifle with no tendency toward a crouching stance. Viewed from behind, the hind legs are parallel, with the hocks turning neither in nor out. Cowhocks or bowed legs are serious faults. The hind feet point straight ahead. Steep, poorly angulated hindquarters are a serious fault. The dewclaws, if any, may be removed.

Tail: The tail is not to be docked, and is set in continuation of the spine with but slight curvature, and carried gaily in hound fashion. The hair on the underside of the tail is coarse.

Size: The height should not exceed 14 inches. Height over 15 inches at the highest point at the shoulder blades is a disqualification.

Gait: The Basset Hound moves in a smooth, powerful, and effortless manner. Being a scenting dog with short legs, it holds its nose low to the ground. Its gait is absolutely true with perfect co-ordination between the front and hind legs, and it moves in a straight line with hind feet following the line with the front feet, the hocks well bent with no stiffness of action. The front legs do not paddle, weave, or overlap, and the elbows must lie close to the body. Going away, the hind legs are parallel.

Coat: The coat is hard, smooth, and short, with sufficient density to be of use in all weather. The skin is loose and elastic. A distinctly long coat is a disqualification.

Color: Any recognized hound color is acceptable and the distribution of color and markings is of no importance.

DISQUALIFICATIONS
Height of more than 15 inches at the highest point of the shoulder blades.
Knuckled over front legs.
Distinctly long coat.
APPROVED JANUARY 14, 1964

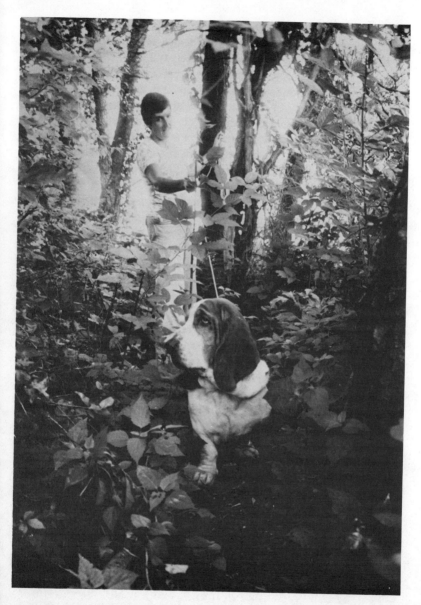

Bassets perform exceptionally well in field trials, and you might consider this sporting pastime if you are willing to invest the necessary time to train your dog. This Basset "performs" at the "hunt 'em up" command of his master, who holds him firmly on lead.

3. FIELD AND OBEDIENCE TRIALS

THE BASSET HOUND AS HUNTER

Before attempting to train a Basset Hound of any age, one does well to contemplate the fact that the breed has been deliberately bred for almost 10 centuries to be exactly the same temperamentally. This means that basically all Bassets are possessed of the same type of thought processes and reactions.

Bred to hunt slowly and carefully and to rely on their noses above any other sense, the Basset Hound has a strong will and is self-reliant to a degree. He cannot be hustled, and one must realize that in reaction the Basset is as slow as he is in motion. When giving a command, do not expect a Fox Terrier response. Your Basset must consider the request, and then get in motion, all of which takes time. Their dependency on their nose is best illustrated by the fact that few Bassets will follow your trail by sight, even if you can be clearly seen. The Basset will put his nose to the ground and trail you carefully. Part of his slowness to react to a command is due to the fact that he must correlate what his eyes see, his ears hear, and his nose smells, before he can make the decision to follow the command. All this is not to be regarded as foolishness. The Basset Hound is one of the finest hunting hounds ever developed, and all these characteristics go into making him superb in the field. Here he is easy to handle because of his gentle and willing nature, and yet he is stronghearted and determined on the trail, seldom confused, and always willing to keep working as long as he is asked to do so. His rugged independence is an integral part of his hunting prowess, because he depends on no man or dog for his information about the trail he is working. His decisions are his own.

ON THE TRAIL

The training of a hound to trail game is not at all complicated. Based on the assumption that your dog has real aptitude for hunting, I will try to set forth a few simple suggestions on how to go about training.

The earlier you start working with your pup, the better. Begin teaching him (or her) to follow a scent by such simple methods as dragging a piece of meat or a bone a few feet, outdoors or in. Take him to the start of the "line," tap the spot you want him to smell, and say, "Hunt

(1) The trainer holds a glove aloft for the Basset Hound to become familiar with. (2) The dog reaches one of the stakes on the tracking field. (3) A layout of tracking paraphernalia, including the stakes with flags atop; a clipboard for record-keeping; glove; lead; etc. In (4), the Basset is allowed to sniff the glove to pick up its scent, and in (5) the dog keeps his nose to the ground as he follows the trails.

1

2

3

4

5

'em up," or "Go find it," or whatever phrase you think you will want to use afield for this order. Lead the pup along the line of the drag, continuing to tap the line and to talk to him encouragingly. Let him have whatever he finds at the end of the trail for a reward.

As soon as you are ready to advance to more extensive training out of doors, buy a tube of training scent for rabbits, and follow the instructions of the manufacturer for its use. Make the line short at first, lengthening it as the pup increases in ability. Never let the pup quit before he has reached the end of this prepared trail. Go along with him as long as it is necessary to see that he stays with it.

Be sure you know exactly where you laid the trail, for nothing undermines a pup's confidence in you, and in himself as much as being corrected when he is right and you are wrong. Do not be concerned if the pup learns to trail a few feet to one side or the other to the track you lay—this is entirely due to the drift of the scent on the wind.

When you start your pup on real game you had better plan to stick near him at first. Take the pup to a clump of grass or alders wherein most likely hides a rabbit. Tell the dog what you told him when he was trailing meat in your kitchen; let him poke around and rout out the rabbit for himself. Once he has found game, he will learn to assume this responsibility and will always do it.

Try to follow the course the rabbit takes, which is a lot easier said than done. Go with your pup, encouraging him on the trail, and if he stops or seems confused, urge him to scout around and try to pick up the trail again. If the rabbit has holed up, tell your pup he is a good boy, lead him away from that spot and try to put up a new quarry.

Sometimes it is possible to have the assistance of a kindly old experienced Basset who will help train a pup. If the dogs are friends your pup will work with the oldtimer and learn much from him. But do not risk working a novice pup with a fast, aggressive young dog, for the pup will become utterly discouraged at being so outclassed.

FIELD TRIALS

Basset Hounds perform exceptionally well in field trials, and you might consider this sport if you are willing to invest the necessary time and patience to train a field competitor.

The first field trial held in America took place in 1937. The first Basset Hound Field Trial champion is one "Hillcrest Peggy," who was owned and trained by Mr. and Mrs. Emil Seitz. From the time of that first field trial up until the present, field trial meets have steadily grown in popularity. These trials are held by various breed clubs, and some are sanctioned by the American Kennel Club. The field trials that you would be interested in entering are those sponsored by the Basset Hound Club of America.

By writing to the American Kennel Club in New York, you can obtain a copy of the booklet entitled "Rules Applying to Registration and Field Trials," which lists the regulations for all the different field trial categories. They include the Member Field Trial, at which a dog may win points towards his championship. Such trials are given by breed clubs and associations which are members of the American Kennel Club. Licensed Field Trials are those at which championship points are also awarded. The sponsoring club of such a trial is not a member of the AKC, but it has authority to run the trial by having been granted a special license by that organization. A Sanctioned Field trial is an informal trial at which dogs are competing not for points toward their championship, but for general experience and practice. Sponsoring clubs may or may not be AKC-members.

These trials usually take up the better part of a weekend, sometimes extending to three days. Before your Basset Hound is ready to compete at one, he will have had to undergone training by you or a professional trainer. The dogs who compete at these trials possess extraordinary skills, which are learned only through thorough and patient training.

You or the professional trainer who is to work with your dog will have basic requirements in regards to training tools. They include: a 50-foot cord with leather handle; "flushing" whip; choke collar; dog bell and whistle; training scent; training dummy; .22 caliber blank cartridge revolver; etc. If you are going to get this involved in the training of your Basset Hound, however, it is strongly advised that you first receive some training yourself from a professional. If you are familiar with hunters, ask them to acquaint you with the training techniques they used to train their dogs for field work. Or, consult your local library, where a wealth of training books is usually available. You can't really be expected to go out into a field with your young Basset totally unprepared, not knowing how to go about instructing him on the finer points of being a "gun dog." Therefore, it is best that you are knowledgeable about all phases of this training before you begin it. There is no substitute for experience when it comes to matters such as the handling of the "training" gun. When the time comes to introduce the gun, begin with the aforementioned .22 caliber blank pistol, and shoot it when the dog is totally engrossed in trailing. Use this blank pistol until you can fire it near the dog under any circumstances without his showing any signs of fear or alarm. When you are ready to introduce the shotgun, be sure the hound is actively trailing and arrange to shoot the rabbit far enough ahead of the dog so that it won't alarm him, yet close enough so that he can connect in his mind the shot and the subsequent encounter with any fresh killed game.

Some Bassets will retrieve without any formal training. Your Basset Hound should not be allowed to eat the rabbit, but it helps fill the dog with the hunting urge to be allowed to smell it thoroughly.

The aforementioned Sanctioned Field Trials provide an excellent opportunity for you and your Basset Hound to become acquainted with the world of field trial competition. These informal meets are an excellent way of acclimating your Basset Hound to the hunting world, and to the thrill of competition.

FIELD AND OBEDIENCE TRIAL PARTICULARS

Each year, many field trials are held throughout the country for Basset Hound competition. If this sort of "hobby" appeals to you, it would be a good idea to inquire at the Basset Hound Club of America for particulars on trials in your area, and for the addresses of local clubs near you. The AKC can furnish the name and address of the national club secretary; the AKC address is in Chapter Four.

Field trial competition for Bassets is divided by sex and experience into separate classes. In "brace" competition, two Bassets are run together, their names being chosen by lot. At the start of each brace, the gallery (field trial assistants) spreads out and walks up a rabbit. The competing dogs are kept leashed during this time, and when the rabbit goes out, they are brought to the spot, and turned loose together. From then on the gallery hangs back so as not to interfere with the dogs, and only the judges and handlers are allowed to follow closely. The judges are responsible for all directions during the running of a brace. They tell you what to do and when to do it. You are not allowed to give your dog any assistance or directions unless told to do so by the judge.

Trials have grown in size until nowadays it is not unusual to have total entries over 100. Any pure bred Basset Hound may compete, as long as he is eligible for AKC registration, and if he is at least six months old. Points towards the title of Field Trial champion are based on the number of competing hounds, and points are awarded to first, second, and third place if the entry is large enough. The number of points needed is changed from time to time as the size of the entries increases.

You will find that field trialers are a sociable and friendly group of people, and your Basset will love every minute of it, doing what he most likes to do—hunting.

Most Bassets accept with such good nature and comprehension all types of training that one has little to do. For instance, if I wish to put a collar and leash on a pup for the first time, chances are he will make a

Your family Basset may appear to want to do nothing else but sleep, but he is actually a vigorous hunter and field trialer, if allowed to pursue the hunting urge that was bred into him.

few modest bucks and kicks, and then off he will go, easy as an old hand. I'll let him go his own way at first, then gradually ease into taking him where I want to go, and there is almost no chore to it. Again, a Basset pup almost invariably sits or lies down every time he stops moving, so that all I have to do is coordinate the command with the act, and soon that lesson is learned.

Obedience courses, while probably better suited to the working breeds, are not by any means beyond the capabilities of the Basset Hound. Providing you allow your pupil to take his time, you will find him a happy and willing worker.

Most obedience training instructions are adjusted to the working breeds which have been especially developed to accept considerable training and to take orders. The Basset Hound, having been bred to be an independent, self-reliant hunter, is not particularly attentive to the orders issued by its owner. While it is frowned upon by dedicated obedience trainers, the use of food as an "assist" in training your Basset is a shortcut and one of the greatest helps in many situations. One often finds that his hound is simply not listening to instructions, but is lost in contemplation. Nothing brings the dog back to earth so quickly as a

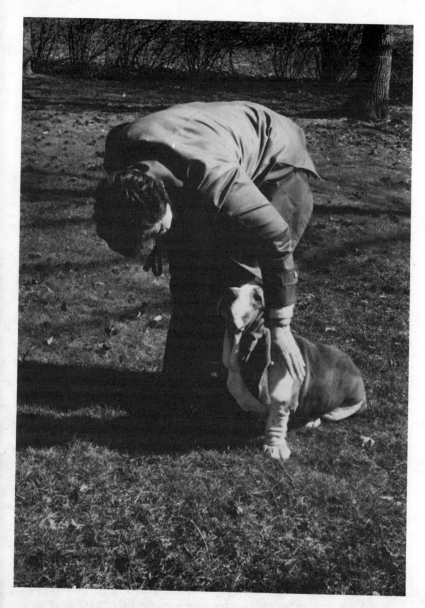

Words of encouragement and a kind pat will help in teaching your Basset Hound the simple obedience commands of "sit," "heel," etc. If you are firm, yet remember to give ample rewards occasionally, you will see good results in training.

This woman teaches her dog the "sit" command, using the appropriate hand signal reinforced with a verbal command. It is important to teach your dog the basic obedience commands, which will make him well-mannered and ensure his safety should he run out onto a busy street. In such a case, your command of "stop" may prevent him from running into traffic.

favorite tidbit. Once you have regained his attention, the lesson can proceed apace.

In as basic a matter as training to walk on the leash, food can solve the problem of the balky or frightened pup. If you walk along, talking encouragingly, passing out bits of food to the puppy now and then, it is amazing to see how quickly he learns to trot along happily with no protest. This is especially vital in a show dog, and the greatest care must be used to create in the puppy's mind only the happiest association with a leash and collar.

A HOME-TAUGHT OBEDIENCE COURSE

A complete obedience course can be taught at home with the help of various excellent training books; however, if you are anxious to compete in trials it is strongly recommended that you and your dog join a course in obedience. The many distractions of group work, strange surroundings, and precise form required for you as trainer all are things which no one can easily reproduce at home.

The keys to success in training any breed of dog are, first, know your own role perfectly so that when the class instructor gives an order, you can obey without hesitation. Sometimes the instructors fail to advise their novice trainers that one always begins an exercise in heeling by

The "heel" command is effected here easily by giving a verbal command. Teach your Basset Hound early on to associate the proper behavior or command with the appropriate verbal message. Don't confuse matters by using different words for the same command: when you want your dog to sit, say "sit," and don't vary it with other words.

leading off with the left foot, as an example. Further, in case the dog is supposed to remain in a "stay" position, one leads off with the right foot. Somehow the dog knows the difference. One must watch to avoid falling into the habit of giving double commands. In a trial this costs many points. By double command is meant, for example, saying "heel," and jerking the lead, and slapping your thigh. It is necessary to turn left, right, and about face with military precision, always the same, to aid your dog in perfecting his handling of these orders.

The second key is to remember always that your Basset Hound is long, fat, and slow, and no matter how eager he is to do what you order, it takes him longer to do it than it does the average dog. You must be extremely patient. And the third key is never lose your temper with your Basset. This breed is extremely sensitive, and once scolded and shaken up for not following an instruction he probably doesn't grasp, the dog will wilt and merely shuffle through the exercises, if indeed he will do them at all. Now that more and more Bassets are taking obedience courses, most instructors are aware of the breed characteristics, and consider them in the instructions given the Basset owner.

4. THE NEW BASSET HOUND PUPPY

PREPARING FOR YOUR BASSET PUPPY'S ARRIVAL

In choosing a puppy, be certain beforehand that each member of the family is truly enthusiastic about having this particular breed of dog as an addition to their circle. Dogs are much too intelligent not to sense whether or not they are liked. If your puppy feels unwanted, you may find an unhappy dog on your hands that could easily turn into a "problem child." Before buying, research the breed and make sure it is the one for you. Besides reading, a good way to learn about your prospective pet is to observe one of the same breed in its permanent home surroundings. Most owners will be only too happy to show off their furry friend.

One of the most important factors to consider when selecting a dog, whether it is to be a pet or show dog, is its temperament. When looking at a litter of puppies for a prospective purchase, spend time just quietly observing them. Usually the most outgoing or aggressive puppy is your best bet. However, do not overlook the more reserved puppy. Most dogs are wary of strangers, so reserve may indicate caution, not timidity. He may calmly accept your presence when he senses that all is well. In any event, never force yourself on a puppy—let him come to you. Beware of the puppy that hides in the corner and won't emerge until you have left. Chances are he will always be high-strung and may develop more undesirable habits as a result of his nervousness.

Because at least three out of four prospective purchasers of dogs want to buy a young rather than an adult or almost adult dog, the problem of preparing for the arrival of a permanent canine house guest almost always means preparing for the arrival of a puppy. This is not to say that there is anything wrong with purchasing an adult dog; on the contrary, such a purchase has definite advantages in that it often allows freedom from housebreaking chores and rigorous feeding schedules, and these are a definite benefit to prospective purchasers who have little time to spare. Since the great majority of dog buyers, however, prefer to watch their pet grow from sprawlingly playful puppyhood to dignified maturity, buying a dog, practically speaking, means buying a puppy. Before you get a puppy be sure that you are willing to take the responsibility of training him and caring for his physical needs. His early training is most important, as an adult dog that is a well-behaved member of the family is the end product of your early training. Remember that your new puppy knows only

41

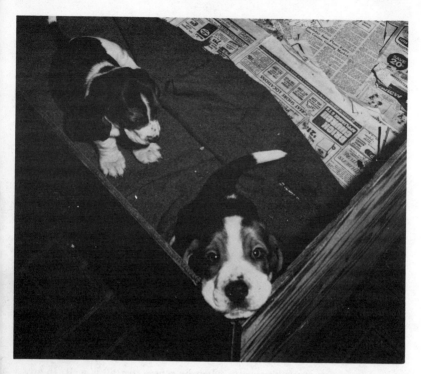

When selecting a Basset, it is often a good bet to select the inquisitive pup who comes bounding up to greet you. The pup who seems curious and active is most likely an alert, healthy one.

a life of romping with his littermates and the security of being with his mother, and that coming into your home is a new and sometimes frightening experience for him. He will adjust quickly if you are patient with him and show him what you expect of him. If there are small children in the family be sure that they do not abuse him or play roughly with him. A puppy plays hard, but he also requires frequent periods of rest. Before he comes, decide where he is to sleep and where he is to eat. If your puppy does not have a collar, find out the size he requires and buy an inexpensive one, as he will soon outgrow it. Have the proper grooming equipment on hand. Consult the person from whom you bought the puppy as to the proper food for your puppy, and learn the feeding time and amount that he eats a day. Buy him some toys—usually the breeder will give you some particular toy or toys which he has cherished as a puppy to add to his new ones and to make him less homesick. Get everything you need from your pet shop before you bring the puppy home.

MALE OR FEMALE?

Before buying your puppy you should have made a decision as to whether you want a male or female. Unless you want to breed your pet and raise a litter of puppies, your preference as to the sex of your puppy is strictly a personal choice. On the whole both sexes are pretty much the same in disposition and character, and both make equally good pets.

SHOW DOG OR PET?

It is well to define in your own mind the purpose for which you want a dog, and to convey this to the breeder. A great deal of disappointment and dissatisfaction can be avoided by a meeting of the minds between seller and buyer.

Although every well-bred healthy member of the breed makes an ideal companion and pet, actual pet stock is usually the least expensive of the purebred registered stock. The person who asks for a pet, pays a pet-geared price for the animal. Pet stock is least expensive because these dogs are deemed unsuitable for breeding or exhibition in comparison to the standard of perfection for the breed. Generally only skilled breeders and judges can point out the structural differences between a pet and show quality dog.

If you are planning to show your dog, make this clear to the breeder and he will aid you in selecting the best possible specimen of the breed. A show quality dog may be more expensive than one meant for a pet, but it will be able to stand up to show ring competition.

WHERE TO BUY YOUR BASSET PUP

Once you have decided on the particular breed that you want for your pet, your task is to find that one special dog from among several outlets. Buying a well-bred, healthy dog is your foremost concern. By doing a little research in the various dog magazines and newspapers you can locate the names and addresses of breeders and kennels in your area that are known for breeding quality animals. The American Kennel Club will also furnish you with addresses of people to contact that are knowledgeable about your chosen breed.

Your local pet shop, although necessarily restricted from carrying all breeds in stock, may sometimes be able to supply quality puppies on demand. Due to the exorbitant amount of space and time needed to properly rear puppies, pet shops generally prefer to assist owners by supplying all the tools and equipment needed in the raising and training of the puppies. The pet shop proprietor, if unable to obtain a dog for you, can often refer you to a reputable kennel with which he has done business before.

SIGNS OF GOOD HEALTH

Picking out a healthy, attractive little fellow to join the family circle is a different matter from picking a show dog: it is also a great deal less complicated. Often the puppy will pick you. If he does, and it is mutual admiration at first sight, he is the best puppy for you. Trust your eyes and hands to tell if the puppy is sound in body and temperament. Ears and eyes should not have suspicious discharges. Legs should have strong bones; bodies should have solid muscles. Coats should be clean. Lift the hair to see that the skin is free of scales and parasites.

Reliable breeders and pet shops will urge you to take your puppy to the veterinarian of your choice to have the puppy's health checked, and will allow you at least two days to have it done. It should be clearly understood whether rejection by a veterinarian for health reasons means that you have the choice of another puppy from that litter or that you get your money back. Be sure to get the details of this policy before you purchase any puppy.

PAPERS

When you buy a purebred dog you should receive his American Kennel Club registration certificate (or an application form to fill out), a pedigree and a health certificate made out by the breeder's veterinarian. The registration certificate is the official A.K.C. paper. If the puppy was named and registered by his breeder you will want to complete the transfer and send it, with the appropriate fee, to the American Kennel Club. They will transfer the dog to your ownership in their records and send you a new certificate. If you receive, instead, an application for registration, you should fill it out choosing a name for your dog, and mail it, with the fee, to the A.K.C.

The pedigree is a chart showing your puppy's ancestry and is not a part of his official papers. The health certificate will tell what shots have been given and when the next ones are due. Your veterinarian will be appreciative of this information, and will continue with the same series of shots, if they have not been completed. The health certificate will also give the date on which the puppy has been wormed.

REGISTERING YOUR BASSET HOUND PUP

For information on how to register a new litter of pedigreed dogs owners may write to the following:

American Kennel Club
51 Madison Ave.
New York, N.Y. 10010

Canadian Kennel Club
111 Eglinton Avenue East
Toronto 12, Ontario
Canada

Australian Kennel Club
Royal Show Grounds
Ascot Vale, Victoria
Australia

British Kennel Club
1 Clarges Street
Picadilly, London W.1
England

THE PUPPY'S FIRST NIGHT WITH YOU

The puppy's first night at home is likely to be disturbing to the family. Keep in mind that suddenly being away from his mother, brothers and sisters is a new experience for him; he may be confused and frightened. If you have a special room in which you have his bed, be sure that there is nothing there with which he can harm himself. Be sure that all lamp cords are out of his reach and that there is nothing that he can tip or pull over. Check furniture that he might get stuck under or behind and objects that he might chew. If you want him to sleep in your room he probably will be quiet all night, reassured by your presence. If left in a room by himself he will cry and howl, and you will have to steel yourself to be impervious to his whining. After a few nights alone he should adjust. The first night that he is alone it is wise to put a loud-ticking alarm clock, as well as his toys, in the room with him. The alarm clock will make a comforting noise, and he will not feel that he is alone.

YOUR PUPPY'S BED

Every dog likes to have a place that is his alone. He holds nothing more sacred than his own bed whether it be a rug, dog crate, or dog bed. If you get your puppy a bed be sure to get one which discourages chewing. Also be sure that the bed is large enough to be comfortable for him when he is full grown. Locate it away from drafts and radiators. A word might be said here in defense of the crate, which many pet owners think is cruel and confining. Given a choice, a young dog instinctively selects a secure place in which to lounge, rest or sleep. The walls and ceiling of a crate, even a wire one, answer that need. Once he regards his crate as a safe and reassuring place to stay, you will be able to leave him alone in the house.

FEEDING YOUR BASSET HOUND PUP

At the time of purchase, most breeders will give you food for a few days, along with instructions for feeding so that your puppy will have the same diet he is accustomed to until you can buy a supply at your pet shop.

As a general rule, a puppy from weaning time (six weeks) to three months of age should be fed four meals a day; from three months to six

1

2

(1) Make sure that your Basset Hound has plenty of fresh water available at all times. Remember, your dog can't *ask* you for a drink when he's thirsty, so see to it that the water is there for him. (2) Every dog, including your Basset, likes a bed of his own. Whether it is an elaborate wicker-and-pillows combination or a cardboard box lined with a fluffy blanket, your Basset will love having his own "digs."

months, three meals; from six months to one year, two meals. After a year, a dog does well on one meal daily. There are as many feeding schedules as there are breeders, and puppies do fine on all of them, so it is best for the new owner to follow the one given him by the breeder of his puppy. Remember that all dogs are individuals. The amount that will keep your dog in good health is right for him, not the "rule book" amount. A feeding schedule to give you some idea of what the average puppy will eat is as follows:

Morning meal: Puppy meal with milk.

Afternoon meal: Meat mixed with puppy meal, plus a vitamin-mineral supplement.

Evening meal: Same as afternoon meal, but without a vitamin-mineral supplement.

Do not change the amounts in your puppy's diet too rapidly. If he gets diarrhea it may be that he is eating too much, so cut back on his food and when he is normal again increase his food more slowly.

There is a canned food made especially for puppies which you can buy with a veterinarian's prescription, and several commercially prepared products. Some breeders use this method very successfully from weaning to three months.

TRANSITIONAL DIET

Changing over to an adult program of feeding is not difficult. Very often the puppy will change himself: that is, he will refuse to eat some of his meals. He'll adjust to his one meal (or two meals) a day without any trouble at all.

BREAKING TO COLLAR AND LEASH

Puppies are usually broken to a collar before you bring them home, but even if yours has never worn one it is a simple matter to get him used to it. Put a loose collar on him for a few hours. At first he may scratch at it and try to get it off, but gradually he will take it as a matter of course. To break him to a lead, attach his leash to his collar and let him drag it around. When he becomes used to it pick it up and gently pull him in the direction you want him to go. He will think it is a game, and with a bit of patience on your part he will allow himself to be led.

DISCIPLINING YOUR PUPPY

The way to have a well-mannered adult dog is to give him firm basic training while he is a puppy. When you say "No" you must mean "No." Your dog will respect you only if you are firm. A six-to eight-week-old puppy is old enough to understand what "No" means. The first time you

If your Basset pup should appear as stubborn as this one does in regards to obeying commands, simply continue training in a firm yet gentle manner. You will find that if you are firm, your Basset will eventually "get the message," and training will be accomplished.

see your puppy doing something he shouldn't be doing, chewing something he shouldn't chew or wandering in a forbidden area, it's time to teach him. Say "No" firmly. Usually a firm "No" in a disapproving tone of voice is enough to correct your dog, but occasionally you get a puppy that requires a firmer hand, especially as he grows older. In this case hold your puppy firmly and slap him gently across the hindquarters. If this seems cruel, you should realize that no dog resents being disciplined if he is caught in the act of doing something wrong, and your puppy will be intelligent enough to know what the slap was for.

After you have slapped him and you can see that he has learned his lesson, call him to you and talk to him in a pleasant tone of voice—praise him for coming to you. This sounds contradictory, but it works with a puppy. He immediately forgives you, practically tells you that it was his fault and that he deserved his punishment, and promises that it will not happen again. This form of discipline works best and may be used for all misbehaviors.

Never punish your puppy by chasing him around, making occasional swipes with a rolled-up newspaper: punish him only when you have a firm hold on him. Above all, never punish your dog after having called him to you. He must learn to associate coming to you with something pleasant.

HOUSEBREAKING

While housebreaking your puppy, do not let him have the run of the house. If you do you will find that he will pick out his own bathroom, which may be in your bedroom or in the middle of the living room rug. Keep him confined to a small area where you can watch him, and you will be able to train him much more easily and speedily. A puppy does not want to dirty his bed, but he does need to be taught where he should go. Spread papers over his living quarters, then watch him carefully. When you notice him starting to whimper, sniff the floor or run agitatedly in little circles, rush him to the place that you want to serve as his relief area and gently hold him there until he relieves himself. Then praise him lavishly. When you remove the soiled papers, leave a small damp piece so that the puppy's sense of smell will lead him back there next time. If he makes a mistake, wash the area at once with warm water, followed by a rinse with water and vinegar or sudsy ammonia. This will kill the odor and prevent discoloration. It shouldn't take more than a few days for him to get the idea of using newspapers. When he becomes fairly consistent, reduce the area of paper to a few sheets in a corner. As soon as you think he has the idea fixed in his mind, you can let him roam around the house a bit, but keep an eye on him. It might be best to keep him on a leash the first few days so that you can rush him back to his paper at any signs of an approaching accident.

The normal healthy puppy will want to relieve himself when he wakes up in the morning, after each feeding and after strenuous exercise. During early puppyhood any excitement, such as the return home of a member of the family or the approach of a visitor, may result in floor-wetting, but that phase should pass in a few weeks. Keep in mind that you can't expect too much from your puppy until he is about five months old. Before that, his muscles and digestive system just aren't under his control.

OUTDOOR HOUSEBREAKING

You can begin outdoor training on a leash even while you are paper-training your puppy. First thing in the morning take him outdoors (to the curb, if you are in the city) and walk him back and forth in a small area until he relieves himself. He will probably make a puddle and then walk around, uncertain of what is expected of him. You can try standing him over a newspaper, which may give him the idea. Praise your dog every time taking him outside brings results, and he will get the idea. You'll find, when you begin the outdoor training, that the male puppy usually requires a longer walk than the female. Both male and female puppies will squat. It isn't until he is older that the male dog will begin to lift his leg. If you hate to give up your sleep, you can train your puppy to go outdoors during the day and use the paper at night.

ALL DOGS NEED TO CHEW

Puppies and young dogs need something with resistance to chew on while their teeth and jaws are developing—for cutting the puppy teeth, to induce growth of the permanent teeth under the puppy teeth, to assist in getting rid of the puppy teeth at the proper time, to help the permanent teeth through the gums, to assure normal jaw development and to settle the permanent teeth solidly in the jaws.

The adult dog's desire to chew stems from the instinct for tooth cleaning, gum massage and jaw exercise—plus the need for an outlet for periodic doggie tensions.

Dental caries as it affects the teeth of humans is virtually unknown in dogs—but tartar accumulates on the teeth of dogs, particularly at the gum line, more rapidly than on the teeth of humans. These accumulations, if not removed, bring irritation, and then infection which erodes the tooth enamel and ultimately destroys the teeth at the roots. Most chewing by adult dogs is an effort to do something about this problem for themselves.

Tooth and jaw development will normally continue until the dog is more than a year old—but sometimes much longer, depending upon the breed, chewing exercise, the rate at which calcium can be utilized and many other factors, known and unknown, which affect the development of individual dogs. Diseases, like distemper for example, may sometimes arrest development of the teeth and jaws, which may resume months, or even years later.

This is why dogs, especially puppies and young dogs, will often destroy property worth hundreds of dollars, when their chewing instinct is not diverted from their owner's possessions, particularly during the widely varying critical period for young dogs.

Saving your possessions from destruction, assuring proper development of teeth and jaws, providing for 'interim' tooth cleaning and gum massage, and channeling doggie tensions into a non-destructive outlet are, therefore, all dependent upon the dog having something suitable for chewing readily available when his instinct tells him to chew. If your purposes, and those of your dog, are to be accomplished, what you provide for chewing must be desirable from the doggie viewpoint, have the necessary functional qualities, and above all, be safe for your dog.

It is very important that dogs not be permitted to chew on anything they can break, or indigestible things from which they can bite sizeable chunks. Sharp pieces, from such as a bone which can be broken by a dog, may pierce the intestine wall and kill. Indigestible things which can be

Nylabone®, a unique 100 percent nylon chew bone, is the perfect chewing pacifier for young dogs in their teething stage, or even for older dogs to help satisfy that occasional urge to chew. Unlike many other dog bones on the market today, Nylabone® does not splinter or fall apart. It will last indefinitely and as it is used it frills, becoming a doggie toothbrush that cleans teeth and massages gums.

bitten off in chunks, such as toys made of rubber compound or cheap plastic, may cause an intestinal stoppage, if not regurgitated—to bring painful death, unless surgery is promptly performed.

Strong natural bones, such as 4 to 8 inch lengths of round shin bone from mature beef—either the kind you can get from your butcher or one of the variety available commercially in pet stores—may serve your dog's teething needs, if his mouth is large enough to handle them effectively.

You may be tempted to give your puppy a smaller bone and he may not be able to break it when you do—but puppies grow rapidly and the power of their jaws constantly increases until maturity. This means that a growing dog may break one of the smaller bones at any time, swallow the pieces and die painfully before you realize what is wrong.

Many people make the mistake of thinking of their dog's teeth in terms of the teeth of the wild carnivores or those of the dog in antiquity. The teeth of the wild carnivorous animals, and the teeth found in the fossils of the dog-like creatures of antiquity, have far thicker and stronger enamel than those of our contemporary dogs.

All hard natural bones are highly abrasive. If your dog is an avid chewer, natural bones may wear away his teeth prematurely; hence, they then should be taken away from your dog when the teething purposes have been served. The badly worn, and usually painful, teeth of many mature dogs can be traced to excessive chewing on natural bones.

Contrary to popular belief, knuckle bones which can be chewed up and swallowed by the dog provide little, if any, useable calcium or other nutriment. They do, however, disturb the digestion of most dogs and cause them to vomit the nourishing food they need.

An old leather shoe is another popular answer to the chewing need—but be very sure that the rubber heel, all nails, and other metal parts such as lace grommets, metal arches, etc., have been removed. Be especially careful to get all of the nails. A chunk of rubber heel can cause an intestinal stoppage. If it has a nail in it, the intestine wall may be pierced or torn. Then there is, of course, always the hazard that your dog may fail to differentiate between his shoe and yours, and eat up a good pair while you're not looking.

Dried rawhide products of various types, shapes, sizes and prices have come on the market during the past few years. They don't serve the primary chewing functions very well, they are a bit messy when wet from mouthing, and most dogs chew them up rather rapidly—but they have been considered safe for dogs until recently. During the past few months, however, a number of cases of death, and near death, by strangulation have been reported to be the result of partially swallowed chunks of rawhide swelling in the throat. More recently, some veterinarians have been attributing cases of acute constipation to large pieces of incompletely digested rawhide in the intestine.

The nylon bones, especially those with natural meat and bone fractions added, are probably the most complete, safe and economical answer to the chewing need. Dogs cannot break them or bite off sizeable chunks; hence, they are completely safe—and being longer lasting than other things offered for the purpose, they are economical.

Hard chewing raises little bristle-like projections on the surface of the nylon bones—to provide effective interim tooth cleaning and vigorous gum massage, much in the same way your tooth brush does it for you. The little projections are raked off and swallowed in the form of thin shavings—but the chemistry of the nylon is such that they break down in the stomach fluids and pass through without effect.

The toughness of the nylon provides the strong chewing resistance needed for important jaw exercise and effective help for the teething functions—but there is no tooth wear because nylon is non-abrasive. Being inert, nylon does not support the growth of microorganisms—and it can be washed in soap and water, or it can be sterilized by boiling or in an autoclave.

Nylabone® is highly recommended by veterinarians as a safe, healthy nylon bone that can't splinter or chip. Instead, Nylabone is frizzled by the dog's chewing action, creating a toothbrush-like surface that cleanses the teeth and massages the gums. Nylabone® and Nylaball®, the only chew products made of flavor-impregnated solid nylon, are available in your local pet shop.

Nothing, however, substitutes for periodic professional attention to your dog's teeth and gums, not any more than your toothbrush can do that for you. Have your dog's teeth cleaned by your veterinarian at least once a year, twice a year is better—and he will be healthier, happier and far more pleasant to live with.

Nylaball®, another fully nylon dog pacifier, is a hygienic chew product that will hold your dog's interest for hours. Impregnated with ham flavor, it is a wholly safe, long-lasting product that cannot endanger your dog's life with the threat of fragments that may become lodged in his throat.

5. OBEDIENCE TRAINING

WHEN TO START TRAINING

You should never begin *serious* obedience training before your dog is seven or eight months old. (Some animal psychologists state that puppies can begin training when seven weeks old, if certain techniques are followed. These techniques, however, are still experimental and should be left to the professional trainer.) While your dog is still in his early puppyhood, concentrate on winning his confidence so he will love and admire you. Basic training can be started at the age of three or four months. He should be taught to walk nicely on a leash, sit and lie down on command, and come when he is called.

YOUR PART IN TRAINING

You must patiently demonstrate to your dog what each word of command means. Guide him with your hands and the training leash, reassuring him with your voice, through whatever routine you are teaching him. Repeat the word associated with the act. Demonstrate again and again to give the dog a chance to make the connection in his mind.

Once he begins to get the idea, use the word of command without any physical guidance. Drill him. When he makes mistakes, correct him, kindly at first, more severely as his training progresses. Try not to lose your patience or become irritated, and never slap him with your hand or the leash during the training session. Withholding praise or rebuking him will make him feel bad enough.

When he does what you want, praise him lavishly with words and with pats. Don't continually reward with dog candy or treats in training. The dog that gets into the habit of performing for a treat will seldom be fully dependable when he can't smell or see one in the offing. When he carries out a command, even though his performance is slow or sloppy, praise him and he will perform more readily the next time.

THE TRAINING VOICE

When you start training your dog, use your training voice, giving commands in a firm, clear tone. Once you give a command, persist until it is obeyed, even if you have to pull the dog to obey you. He must learn that training is different from playing, that a command once given must be obeyed no matter what distractions are present. Remember that the tone and pitch of your voice, not loudness, are the qualities that will influence your dog most.

Be consistent in the use of words during training. Confine your commands to as few words as possible and never change them. It is best for only one person to carry on the dog's training, because different people will use different words and tactics that will confuse your dog. The dog who hears "come," "get over here," "hurry up," "here, Rex," and other commands when he is wanted will become totally confused.

TRAINING LESSONS

Training is hard on the dog and the trainer. A young dog just cannot take more than ten minutes of training at a stretch, so limit the length of your first lessons. Then you can gradually increase the length of time to about thirty minutes. You'll find that you too will tend to become impatient when you stretch out a training lesson. If you find yourself losing your temper, stop and resume the lesson at another time. Before and after each lesson have a play period, but don't play during a training session. Even the youngest dog soon learns that schooling is a serious matter; fun comes afterward.

Don't spend too much time on one phase of training, or the dog will become bored. Always try to end a lesson on a pleasant note. Actually, in nine cases out of ten, if your dog isn't doing what you want it's because you're not getting the idea over to him properly.

YOUR TRAINING EQUIPMENT AND ITS USE

The leash is more properly called the lead, so we'll use that term here. The best leads for training are the six-foot webbed-cloth leads, usually olive-drab in color, and the six-foot leather lead. Fancier leads are available and may be used if desired.

You'll need a metal-link collar, called a choke chain, consisting of a metal chain with rings on each end. Even though the name may sound frightening, it won't hurt your dog, and it is an absolute MUST in training. There is a right and a wrong way to put the training collar on. It should go around the dog's neck so that you can attach the lead to the ring at the end of the chain which passes over, not under the neck. It is most important that the collar is put on properly so it will tighten when the lead is pulled and ease when you relax your grip.

The correct way to hold the lead is also very important, as the collar should have some slack in it at all times, except when correcting. Holding the loop in your right hand, extend your arm out to the side, even with your shoulder. With your left hand, grasp the lead as close as possible to the collar, without making it tight. The remaining portion of the lead can

Your local pet store is the source of a large selection of leads and collars that can be used for training or showing, or just taking your pet for a walk. Since puppies quickly outgrow their first collars and leads, plan to purchase at least two sets of equipment.

be made into a loop which is held in the right hand. Keep this arm close to your body. Most corrections will be made with the left hand by giving the lead a jerk in the direction you want the dog to go.

HEELING

"Heeling" in dog language means having your dog walk alongside you on your left side, close to your leg, on lead or off. With patience and effort you can train your dog to walk with you even on a crowded street or in the presence of other dogs.

Now that you have learned the correct way to put on your dog's collar and how to hold the lead, you are ready to start with his first lesson in heeling. Make the dog sit at your left side. Using the dog's name and the command "Heel," start forward on your LEFT foot, giving a tug on the lead to get the dog started. Always use the dog's name first, followed by the command, such as "Rex, heel." Saying his name will help get his attention and will let him know that you are about to give a command.

Walk briskly, with even steps, going around in a large circle, square or straight line. While walking, make sure that your dog stays on the left side and close to your leg. If he lags behind, snap gently on the lead to get him up to you, then praise him lavishly for doing well. If he forges ahead or swings wide, stop and jerk the lead sharply and bring him back to the proper position. Always praise him when he returns to the correct place. As soon as you have snapped the lead to correct your dog, let it go slack again at the desired length. Don't drag the dog or keep the lead taut as this will develop into a tug of war which is ineffective.

To keep your dog's attention, talk to him as you keep him in place. You can also do a series of fast about-turns, giving the lead a jerk as you turn. He will gradually learn that he must pay attention or be jerked to your side. You can vary the routine by changing speeds, doing turns, figure-eights, and by zig-zagging across the training area.

"HEEL" MEANS "SIT," TOO

To the dog, the command "Heel" will also mean that he has to sit in the heel position at your left side when you stop walking with no additional command from you. As you practice heeling, make him sit whenever you stop, at first using the word "Sit," then with no command at all. He'll soon get the idea and sit down when you stop and wait for the command "Heel" to start walking again.

TRAINING TO SIT

Training your dog to sit should be fairly easy. Stand him on your left side, holding the lead fairly short, and command him to "Sit." As you give the verbal command, pull up slightly with the lead and push his hindquarters down. Do not let him lie down or stand up. If he does lie down, snap up on the lead until he rises to a sitting position again. If he is slow to respond, tug more sharply until he has done what you want him to. Keep him in a sitting position for a moment, then release the pressure on the lead and praise him. Constantly repeat the command as you hold him in a sitting position, thus fitting the word to the action in his mind. If he moves at all, immediately repeat the command and press him into a sitting position. After a time he will begin to get the idea and will sit without having to push his hindquarters down. When he reaches that stage, insist that he sit on command. Praise him often, always rewarding a correct action with your praise and affection.

THE "LIE DOWN" OR "DOWN"

The object of this is to get the dog to lie down either on the verbal command "Down" or when you give the hand signal, your hand raised in front of you, palm down. However, until the dog is really sure of the meaning of the command, and will do it by himself with no forcible action from you, the hand signal should only be used to accompany the verbal command. This command may be more difficult at first because it places the dog in a defenseless position, which may cause him to bolt away. Be lavish with your praise and affection when he has assumed the correct position and he will soon learn that nothing bad happens to him, and on the contrary will associate the "Down" position with pleasing his master or mistress.

Don't start training to lie down until the dog is almost letter-perfect in sitting on command. Place the dog in a sit, and kneel before him. With both hands, reach forward to his legs and take one front leg in each hand, thumbs up, holding just above the elbows. Lift his legs slightly off the ground and pull them somewhat out in front of him. Simultaneously, give the command "Down" and lower his front legs to the ground.

Hold the dog down and stroke him to let him know that staying down is what you want him to do. This method is far better than forcing a young dog down. Using force can cause him to become very frightened and he will begin to dislike any training. Always talk to your dog and let him know that you are very pleased with him, and soon you will find that you have a happy working dog.

After he begins to get the idea, slide the lead under your left foot and give the command "Down." At the same time, pull the lead. This will help get the dog down. Meanwhile, raise your hand in the down signal. Don't expect to accomplish all this in one session. Be patient and work with the dog. He'll cooperate if you show him just what you expect him to do.

THE "STAY"

The next step is to train your dog to stay either in a "Sit" or "Down" position. As before, use the lead to teach this command until your dog is responding perfectly to your instruction, then you may try it off the lead. To begin with the Sit-Stay, place your dog in a sitting position beside you in the automatic heel-sit position. Holding the leash in one hand (most trainers prefer the left), take a long step forward and turn to face him holding your free hand open, palm toward him, fingers pointing downward, in front of his nose and speak the command "Stay." If he offers to follow you, as it would be natural for him to do since this has been his ready position for heel, snap up on the lead to return him to the sit, put your hand in front of his face and repeat the command firmly once more. Allow him to remain sitting for a few seconds before going through the procedure again. Each time he successfully performs, praise him profusely and show him you are pleased with him.

Repeat this procedure until your dog behaves as if he understands what is expected of him. When he has mastered this procedure, step away to the right of him, then behind, then a few steps forward, a few steps to the side, and so on, until you have gone the full length of the leash. Anytime your dog offers to follow you, snap upward on the leash, extending your arm palm forward to him and repeat the command sharply. When he has demonstrated a willingness to remain in the correct position while you walk the full extent of the lead, you are ready to train him to remain in position using a longer length of cord, about 25 or 30 feet, and finally the Sit-Stay off the lead.

Once the Sit-Stay is learned, you can teach the Down-Stay by beginning with the Down command, then apply approximately the same methods as in the Sit-Stay.

THE COME ON COMMAND

You can train your dog to come when you call him if you begin when he is young. At first, work with him on lead. Sit the dog, then back away the length of the lead and call him, putting into your voice as much coaxing affection as possible. Give an easy tug on the lead to get him started. When he does come, make a big fuss over him—it might help at this point to give him a small piece of dog candy or food as a reward. He should get the idea soon. You can also move away from him the full length of the lead and call to him something like "Rex, come," then run backward a few steps and stop, making him sit directly in front of you.

Don't be too eager to practice coming on command off lead. Wait until you are certain that you have the dog under perfect control before you try calling him when he's free. Once he gets the idea that he can disobey a command and get away with it, your training program will suffer a serious setback. Keep in mind that your dog's life may depend on his immediate response to a command to come when he is called. If he disobeys off lead, put the lead back on and correct him severely with jerks of the lead.

TEACHING TO COME TO HEEL

The object of this is for you to stand still, say "Heel," and have your dog come right over to you and sit by your left knee in the heel position. If your dog has been trained to sit without command every time you stop, he's ready for this step.

Sit him in front of and facing you and step back one step. Moving only your left foot, pull the dog behind you, then step forward and pull him around until he is in a heel position. You can also have the dog go around by passing the lead behind your back. Use your left heel to straighten him out if he begins to sit behind you or crookedly. This may take a little work, but he will get the idea if you show him just what you want.

THE STAND

Your dog should be trained to stand in one spot without moving his feet, and he should allow a stranger to run his hand over his body and legs without showing any resentment or fear. Employ the same method you used in training him to stay on the sit and down. While walking, place your left hand out, palm toward his nose, and command him to stay. His first impulse will be to sit, so be prepared to stop him by placing your hand under his body, near his hindquarters, and holding him until he gets the idea that this is different from the command to sit. Praise him for standing, then walk to the end of the lead. Correct him strongly if he starts to move. Have a stranger approach him and run his hands over the dog's back and down his legs. Keep him standing until you come back to him. Walk around him from his left side, come to the heel position, and make sure that he does not sit until you command him to. This is a very valuable exercise. If you plan to show your dog, he will have to learn to stand in a show pose and allow the judge to examine him. The judge will run his hands along the dog's back and down the legs, so it is important that the dog stands calmly and steadfastly.

TRAINING SCHOOLS AND CLASSES

There are dog training schools in all parts of the country, some sponsored by the local humane society.

If you feel that you lack the time or the skill to train your dog yourself, there are professional dog trainers who will do it for you, but basically dog training is a matter of training YOU and your dog to work together as a team, and if you don't do it yourself you will miss a lot of fun. Don't give up after trying unsuccessfully for a short time. Try a little harder and you and your dog will be able to work things out.

ADVANCED TRAINING AND OBEDIENCE TRIALS

Once you begin training your dog and you see how well he does, you'll probably be bitten by the "obedience bug"—the desire to enter him in obedience trials held under American Kennel Club auspices.

The A.K.C. obedience trials are divided into three classes: Novice, Open and Utility.

In trials for advanced obedience degrees, your dog will have to successfully accomplish two scent discrimination exercises. From among several objects like the ones above, he will have to choose the one that has been touched by his handler or owner and carries that person's scent.

In the Novice Class the dog will be judged on the following basis:

TEST MAXIMUM SCORE

Heel on lead 40
Stand for examination 30
Heel free—off lead 40
Recall (come on command) 30
One-minute sit (handler in ring) 30
Three-minute down (handler in ring) 30
Maximum total score 200

If the dog "qualifies" in three shows by earning at least 50% of the points for each test, with a total of at least 170 for the trial, he has earned the Companion Dog degree and the letters C.D. (Companion Dog) are entered after his name in the American Kennel Club records.

The hurdle is used in different events in advanced obedience competition. It figures in the single jump, in the retrieve, and in the directed jump. The bar is adjustable, so that the height a dog must jump to successfully accomplish the particular exercise will be proportional to his size. Informal hurdles can be simulated out of a variety of different items for backyard or indoor practice before the actual trial.

After the dog has earned his Companion Dog title, he is eligible to enter the Open Class competition and compete for his next degree. He will be judged on this basis:

TEST MAXIMUM SCORE

Heel free 40
Drop on recall 30
Retrieve (wooden dumbbell) on flat 20
Retrieve over obstacle (hurdle) 30
Broad jump 20
Three-minute sit (handler out of ring) 30
Five-minute down (handler out of ring) 30
Maximum total score 200

Again he must qualify in three shows for the C.D.X. (Companion Dog Excellent) title, earning at least 50% of the points for each test, with a total of at least 170 for the trial. He is then eligible to compete in the Utility Class, where he can earn the Utility Dog (U.D.) degree in these rugged tests:

TEST MAXIMUM SCORE

Scent discrimination (picking up article handled by master
  from group) Article 1 30
Scent discrimination Article 2 30
Directed Retrieve 30
Signal exercise (heeling, etc., on hand signal) 40
Directed jumping (over hurdle and bar jump) 40
Group examination 30
Maximum total score 200

For more complete information about these obedience trials, write for the American Kennel Club's *Regulations and Standards for Obedience Trials*. Dogs that are disqualified from breed shows because of neutering or physical defects are eligible to compete in these trials. Besides the formal A.K.C. obedience trials, there are informal "match" trials in which dogs compete for ribbons and inexpensive trophies. These shows are run by many local fanciers' clubs and by all-breed obedience clubs. In many localities the humane society and other groups conduct their own obedience shows. Your local newspaper, pet shop proprietor or kennel club can keep you informed about such shows in your vicinity, and you will find them listed in the different dog magazines or in the pet column of your paper.

6. BREEDING YOUR DOG

THE QUESTION OF SPAYING

If you feel that you will never want to raise a litter of purebred puppies, and if you do not wish to risk the possibility of an undesirable mating and surplus mongrel puppies inevitably destined for euthanasia at the local pound, you may want to have your female spayed. Spaying is generally best performed after the female has passed her first heat and before her first birthday; this allows the female to attain the normal female characteristics, while still being young enough to avoid the possible complications encountered when an older female is spayed. A spayed female will remain a healthy, lively pet. You often hear that an altered female will become very fat. However, if you cut down on her food intake, she will not gain weight.

On the other hand, if you wish to show your dog in American Kennel Club competition (altered females are disqualified) or enjoy the excitement and feeling of accomplishment of breeding and raising a litter of quality puppies, particularly in your breed and from your pet, then do not spay your dog until a more appropriate time.

Male dogs are almost never altered (castrated) unless they exhibit excessive sexual tendencies.

SEXUAL PHYSIOLOGY

Females usually reach sexual maturity (indicated by the first heat cycle, or season) at eight or nine months of age, but sexual maturity may occur as early as six months or as late as thirteen months of age. Generally, the larger the breed is the longer it takes to reach full maturity.

The average heat cycle (estrus period) lasts for twenty or twenty-one days, and occurs approximately every six months. For about five days immediately preceeding the heat period, the female generally displays restlessness and an increased appetite. The vulva, or external genitals, begins to swell. The discharge, which is bright red at the onset and gradually becomes pale pink to straw in color, increases in quantity for several days and then slowly subsides, finally ceasing altogether. The vaginal discharge is subject to much variation; in some bitches it is quite heavy, in others it may never appear, and in some it may be so slight as to go unnoticed.

About eight or nine days after the first appearance of the discharge, the female becomes very playful with other dogs, but will not allow a mating

Reproductive system of a male dog: 1. Prostate 2. Rectum 3. Anus 4. Section of pelvic bone 5. Testicle 6. Scrotum 7. Bulb (part of Penis) 8. Penis 9. Sheath 10. Vas deferens 11. Bladder.

to take place. Anywhere from the tenth or eleventh day to the seventeenth or eighteenth day, the female will accept males and be able to conceive. Many biologists apply the term "heat" only to this receptive phase rather than to the whole estrus period, as is commonly done by dog fanciers.

The ova (egg cells) from the female's ovaries are discharged into the oviduct toward the close of the acceptance phase, usually the sixteenth to eighteenth day. From the eighteenth day until the end of the cycle, the female is still attractive to males, but she will repulse their advances. The entire estrus, however, may be quite variable; in some females vaginal bleeding ends and mating begins on the fourth day; in others the discharge may continue throughout the entire cycle and the female will not accept males until the seventeenth day or even later.

The male dog—simply referred to by fanciers as the "dog" or "stud," in contrast to the female, which is referred to as the "bitch"—upon reaching sexual maturity, usually at about six to eight months, is able,

Reproductive system of the bitch: 1. Vulva 2. Anus 3. Rectum 4. Uterus 5. Kidney 6. Ovary 7. Ribs (indicated) 8. Developing embryo 9. Vagina.

like other domesticated mammals, to breed at any time throughout the year.

The testes, the sperm-producing organs of the male, descend from the body cavity into the scrotum at birth. The condition of cryptorchidism refers to the retention of one or both testes within the body cavity. A testicle retained within the body cavity is in an environment too hot for it to function normally. A retained testicle may also become cancerous. If only one testicle descends, the dog is known as a monorchid; if neither descends, the dog is known as an anorchid (dog fanciers, however, refer to a dog with the latter condition as a cryptorchid). A monorchid dog is a fertile animal; an anorchid is sterile.

The male dog's penis has a bulbous enlargement at its base and, in addition, like the penis of a number of other mammals, contains a bone. When mating occurs, pressure on the penis causes a reflex action that fills the bulb with blood, swelling it to five times its normal size within the female. This locks, or ties, the two animals together. After ejaculation, the animals usually remain tied for fifteen to thirty minutes. However, they may separate very quickly or remain together an hour or more, depending on the length of time for the blood to drain from the bulb.

CARE OF THE FEMALE IN ESTRUS

If you have a dog-proof run within your yard, it will be safe to leave your female in season there; if you don't have such a run, she should be shut indoors. Don't leave her alone outside even for a minute; she should be exercised only on lead. If you want to prevent the neighborhood dogs from congregating around your doorstep, as they inevitably will as soon as they discover that your female is in season, take her some distance from the house before you let her relieve herself. Take her in your car to a park or field for a chance to "stretch" her legs (always on lead, of course). Keep watch for male dogs, and if one approaches take the female back to the car. After the three weeks are up you can let her out as before with no worry that she can have puppies until her next season.

Some owners find it simpler to board their female at a kennel until her season is over. However, it really is not difficult to watch your female at home. There are various products on the market which are useful at this time. Although the female in season keeps herself quite clean, sometimes she unavoidably stains furniture or rugs. You can buy sanitary belts made expecially for dogs at your pet shop. Consult your veterinarian for information on pills to be taken to check odor during this period. There also is a pill that prevents the female from coming in season for extended periods, and there are many different types of liquids, powders and sprays of varying efficiency used to keep male dogs away. However, the

There are several products on the market designed to make life easier for both you and your bitch during the estrus cycle. Sanitary pads for dogs are one of these items and come complete with a belt for holding the pad in place.

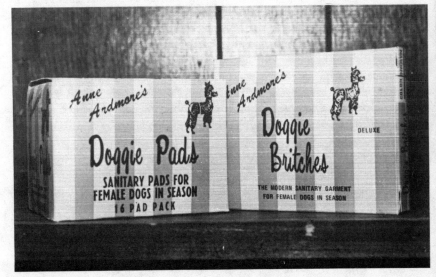

one safe rule (whatever products you use) is: keep your bitch away from dogs that could mount her.

SHOULD YOU BREED YOUR MALE?

Deciding whether or not to use a male dog as a stud is a question with two sides. The arguments for and against using a dog as a stud are often very close to ridiculous. A classic example would be the tale that once you use a dog as a stud he will lose his value as a show dog or any one of the other functions a dog may have. A sound rule may well be: if you have a stud who has proven his worth at the shows, place his services out for hire, if only for the betterment of the breed; if your dog is not of show quality, do not use him as a stud.

Top champion studs can bring their owners many dollars in breeding revenue. If the stud is as good as you feel he is, his services will soon be in great demand. Using a dog as a stud will not lower his value in other functions in any way. Many breeders will permit a male dog to breed an experienced female once, when about a year old, and then they begin to show their stud until he has gained his conformation championship. He is then placed out for hire through advertising in the various bulletins, journals and show catalogues, and through the stud registers maintained by many pet shops and kennel clubs.

SHOULD YOU BREED YOUR FEMALE?

If you are an amateur and decide to breed your female it would be wise to talk with a breeder and find out all that breeding and caring for puppies entails. You must be prepared to assume the responsibility of caring for the mother through her pregnancy and for the puppies until they are of saleable age. Raising a litter of puppies can be a rewarding experience, but it means work as well as fun, and there is no guarantee of financial profit. As the puppies grow older and require more room and care, the amateur breeder, in desperation, often sells the puppies for much less than they are worth; sometimes he has to give them away. If the cost of keeping the puppies will drain your finances, think twice.

If you have given careful consideration to all these things and still want to breed your female, remember that there is some preparation necessary before taking this step.

WHEN TO BREED

It is usually best to breed in the second or third season of your bitch. Consider when the puppies will be born and whether their birth and later care will interfere with your work or vacation plans. Gestation period is approximately fifty-eight to sixty-five days. Allow enough time to select

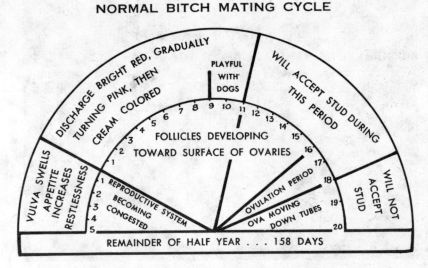

DISCHARGE BRIGHT RED, GRADUALLY TURNING PINK, THEN CREAM COLORED

PLAYFUL WITH DOGS

WILL ACCEPT STUD DURING THIS PERIOD

FOLLICLES DEVELOPING TOWARD SURFACE OF OVARIES

VULVA SWELLS APPETITE INCREASES RESTLESSNESS

REPRODUCTIVE SYSTEM BECOMING CONGESTED

OVULATION PERIOD OVA MOVING DOWN TUBES

WILL NOT ACCEPT STUD

REMAINDER OF HALF YEAR . . . 158 DAYS

the right stud for her. Don't be in a position of having to settle for any available stud if she comes into season sooner than expected. Your female will probably be ready to breed twelve days after the first colored discharge. You can usually make arrangements to board her with the owner of the male for a few days to insure her being there at the proper time, or you can take her to be mated and bring her home the same day. If she still appears receptive she may be bred again a day or two later. Some females never show signs of willingness, so it helps to have the experience of a breeder. The second day after the discharge changes color is the proper time; she may be bred for about three days following. For an additional week or so she may have some discharge and attract other dogs by her odor, but she can seldom be bred at this time.

HOW TO SELECT A STUD

Choose a mate for your female with an eye to countering her deficiencies. If possible, both male and female should have several ancestors in common within the last two or three generations, as such combinations generally "click" best. The male should have a good show record himself or be the sire of champions. The owner of the stud usually charges a fee for the use of the dog. The fee varies. Payment of a fee does not guarantee a litter, but it does generally confer the right to breed your female again to the stud if she does not have puppies the first time. In some cases the owner of the stud will agree to take a choice puppy in place of the stud fee. You and the owner of the stud should settle all details beforehand, including such questions as what age the puppies should reach before the

Maintenance of a state of excellent health is essential if you are contemplating breeding your bitch or stud. Poor health may not only interfere with reproductive processes but can actually rob your dog of his or her interest in mating. If you are not confident in commercial preparations, consult your vet for the best vitamin supplements to add to your dog's diet.

stud's owner can make his choice, what disposition is made of the single surviving puppy under an agreement by which the stud owner has the pick of the litter, and so on. In all cases, it is best that all agreements entered into by bitch owner and stud owner be in the form of a written contract.

It is customary for the female to be sent to the male. If the stud dog of your choice lives any distance from you, you will have to make arrangements to have your female shipped to him. The quickest way is by air, and if you call your nearest airport the airline people will give you information as to the best and fastest flight. Some airlines furnish their own crates for shipping, whereas others require that you furnish your own. The owner of the stud will make the arrangements for shipping the female back to you. You have to pay all shipping charges.

PREPARATION FOR BREEDING

Before you breed your female, make sure she is in good health. She should be neither too thin nor too fat. Skin diseases must be cured before breeding; a bitch with skin diseases can pass them on to her puppies. If

Perpetual Whelping Chart

	Days
Bred—Jan.	1 2 3 4 5 6 7 8 9 10 11 12 13 14 15 16 17 18 19 20 21 22 23 24 25 26 27 28 29 30 31
Due—March	5 6 7 8 9 10 11 12 13 14 15 16 17 18 19 20 21 22 23 24 25 26 27 28 29 30 31 — **April** 1 2 3 4
Bred—Feb.	1 2 3 4 5 6 7 8 9 10 11 12 13 14 15 16 17 18 19 20 21 22 23 24 25 26 27 28
Due—April	5 6 7 8 9 10 11 12 13 14 15 16 17 18 19 20 21 22 23 24 25 26 27 28 29 30 — **May** 1 2
Bred—Mar.	1 2 3 4 5 6 7 8 9 10 11 12 13 14 15 16 17 18 19 20 21 22 23 24 25 26 27 28 29 30 31
Due—May	3 4 5 6 7 8 9 10 11 12 13 14 15 16 17 18 19 20 21 22 23 24 25 26 27 28 29 30 31 — **June** 1 2
Bred—Apr.	1 2 3 4 5 6 7 8 9 10 11 12 13 14 15 16 17 18 19 20 21 22 23 24 25 26 27 28 29 30
Due—June	3 4 5 6 7 8 9 10 11 12 13 14 15 16 17 18 19 20 21 22 23 24 25 26 27 28 29 30 — **July** 1 2
Bred—May	1 2 3 4 5 6 7 8 9 10 11 12 13 14 15 16 17 18 19 20 21 22 23 24 25 26 27 28 29 30 31
Due—July	3 4 5 6 7 8 9 10 11 12 13 14 15 16 17 18 19 20 21 22 23 24 25 26 27 28 29 30 31 — **Aug.** 1 2
Bred—June	1 2 3 4 5 6 7 8 9 10 11 12 13 14 15 16 17 18 19 20 21 22 23 24 25 26 27 28 29 30
Due—August	3 4 5 6 7 8 9 10 11 12 13 14 15 16 17 18 19 20 21 22 23 24 25 26 27 28 29 30 31 — **Sept.** 1
Bred—July	1 2 3 4 5 6 7 8 9 10 11 12 13 14 15 16 17 18 19 20 21 22 23 24 25 26 27 28 29 30 31
Due—September	2 3 4 5 6 7 8 9 10 11 12 13 14 15 16 17 18 19 20 21 22 23 24 25 26 27 28 29 30 — **Oct.** 1 2
Bred—Aug.	1 2 3 4 5 6 7 8 9 10 11 12 13 14 15 16 17 18 19 20 21 22 23 24 25 26 27 28 29 30 31
Due—October	3 4 5 6 7 8 9 10 11 12 13 14 15 16 17 18 19 20 21 22 23 24 25 26 27 28 29 30 31 — **Nov.** 1 2
Bred—Sept.	1 2 3 4 5 6 7 8 9 10 11 12 13 14 15 16 17 18 19 20 21 22 23 24 25 26 27 28 29 30
Due—November	3 4 5 6 7 8 9 10 11 12 13 14 15 16 17 18 19 20 21 22 23 24 25 26 27 28 29 30 — **Dec.** 1 2
Bred—Oct.	1 2 3 4 5 6 7 8 9 10 11 12 13 14 15 16 17 18 19 20 21 22 23 24 25 26 27 28 29 30 31
Due—December	3 4 5 6 7 8 9 10 11 12 13 14 15 16 17 18 19 20 21 22 23 24 25 26 27 28 29 30 31 — **Jan.** 1 2
Bred—Nov.	1 2 3 4 5 6 7 8 9 10 11 12 13 14 15 16 17 18 19 20 21 22 23 24 25 26 27 28 29 30
Due—January	3 4 5 6 7 8 9 10 11 12 13 14 15 16 17 18 19 20 21 22 23 24 25 26 27 28 29 30 31 — **Feb.** 1
Bred—Dec.	1 2 3 4 5 6 7 8 9 10 11 12 13 14 15 16 17 18 19 20 21 22 23 24 25 26 27 28 29 30 31
Due—February	2 3 4 5 6 7 8 9 10 11 12 13 14 15 16 17 18 19 20 21 22 23 24 25 26 27 28 — **March** 1 2 3 4

she has worms she should be wormed before being bred, or within three weeks afterward. It is a good idea to have your veterinarian give her a booster shot for distemper and hepatitis before the puppies are born. This will increase the immunity the puppies receive during their early, most vulnerable period. Choose a dependable veterinarian and rely on him if there is an emergency when your female whelps.

Do not breed your bitch after she reaches six years of age. If you wish to breed her several times while she is young, it is wise to breed her only once a year. In other words, breed her, skip at least one season, and then breed her again. This will allow her to gain back her full strength between whelpings.

THE IMPORTANCE AND APPLICATION OF GENETICS

Any person attempting to breed dogs should have a basic understanding of the transmission of traits, or characteristics, from the parents to the offspring and some familiarity with the more widely used genetic terms that he will probably encounter. A knowledge of the fundamental mechanics of genetics enables a breeder to better comprehend the passing on of good traits and bad from generation to generation and how a stud and bitch either complement or detract from each other's traits. It enables him to make a more judicial and scientific decision in selecting potential mates.

Inheritance, fundamentally, is due to the existence of microscopic units, known as *GENES*, present in the cells of all individuals. Genes somehow control the biochemical reactions that occur within the embryo or adult organism. This control results in changing or guiding the development of the organism's characteristics. A "string" of attached genes is known as a *CHROMOSOME*. With a few important exceptions, every chromosome has a partner chromosome carrying a duplicate or equivalent set of genes. Each gene, therefore, has a partner gene, known as an *ALLELE*. The number of different pairs of chromosomes present in the cells of the organism varies with the type of organism; a certain parasitic worm has only one pair, a certain fruit fly has four different pairs, man has 23 different pairs and your dog has 39 different pairs per cell. Because each chromosome may have many hundreds of genes, a single cell of the body may contain a total of several thousand genes. Heredity is obviously a very complex matter.

In the simplest form of genetic inheritance, one particular gene and its duplicate, or allele, on the partner chromosome control a single characteristic. The presence of freckles in the human skin, for example, is believed to be due to the influence of a single pair of genes.

Each cell of the body contains the specific number of paired

FERTILIZATION

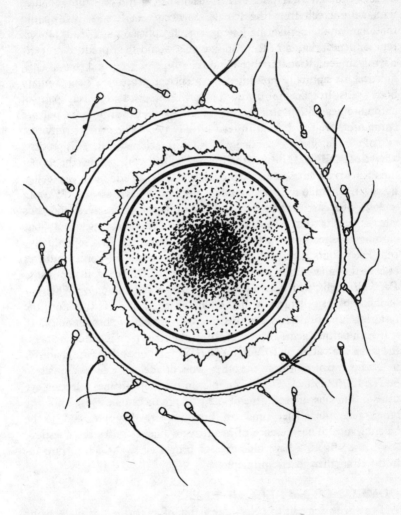

An egg, a special giant cell which the female ovaries produce, is being assaulted by sperm which are attempting to pierce the outer layer of the cell. Only one sperm cell penetration is necessary for fertilization. The first sperm to enter and reach the nucleus will bring with it the necessary chromosomes which will unite with those of the egg. With this union, the full complement of chromosomes necessary for the creation of a new fetus is complete. No other sperm cells are now able to penetrate the egg.

chromosomes characteristic of the organism. Because each type of gene is present on both chromosomes of a chromosome pair, each type of gene is therefore present in duplicate. The fusion of a sperm cell from the male with an egg cell from the female, as occurs in fertilization, should therefore result in offspring having a quadruplicate number (4) of each type of gene. Mating of these individuals would then produce progeny having an octuplicate number (8) of each type of gene, and so on. This, however, is normally prevented by a special process. When ordinary body cells prepare to divide to form more tissue, each pair of chromosomes duplicates itself so that there are four partner chromosomes of each kind instead of only two. When the cell divides, two of the four partners, or one pair, go into each new cell. This process, known as *MITOSIS*, insures that each new body cell contains the proper number of chromosomes. Reproductive cells (sperm and egg cells), however, undergo a special kind of division known as *MEIOSIS*. In meiosis, the chromosome pairs do not duplicate themselves, and thus when the reproductive cells reach the final dividing stage only one chromosome, or one-half of the pair, goes into each new reproductive cell. Each reproductive cell, therefore, has only half the normal number of chromosomes. These are referred to as *HAPLOID* cells, in contrast to *DIPLOID* cells, which have the full number of chromosomes. When the haploid sperm cell fuses with the haploid egg cell in fertilization, the resulting offspring has the normal diploid number of chromosomes.

If both partner genes, or alleles, affect the trait in an identical manner, the genes are said to be *HOMOZYGOUS*, but if one affects the character in a manner different from the other gene, or allele, the genes are said to be *HETEROZYGOUS*. For example, in the pair of genes affecting eye color in humans, if each gene of the pair produces blue eyes, while the other gene, or allele, produces brown eyes, they are said to be heterozygous. The presence of heterozygous genes raises the question, "Will the offspring have blue eyes or brown eyes?" which in turn introduces another genetic principle.

DOMINANCE and RECESSIVENESS

If one gene of a pair can block the action of its partner, or allele, while still producing its own effect, that gene is said to be dominant over its allele. Its allele, on the other hand, is said to be recessive. In the case of heterozygous genes for eye color, the brown eye gene is dominant over the recessive blue eye gene, and the offspring therefore will have brown eyes. Much less common is the occurrence of gene pairs in which neither gene is completely dominant over the other. This, known as IN-COMPLETE or PARTIAL DOMINANCE, results in a blending of the

SIRE and DAM	PROGENY

MENDELIAN EXPECTATION CHART

Pictured are the six possible ways in which a pair of genes can unite. The white boxes represent dominant genes; the black boxes represent recessives. Half of the genes of the sire will unite with half of the genes of the dam, and the expected results of such a mating are shown in the progeny combinations. Ratios apply to expectancy over large litters, except in lines 1, 2 and 6 where expectancy is realized in every litter (the exception due to mutation).

opposing influences. In cattle, if a homozygous (pure) red bull is mated with a homozygous (pure) white cow, the calf will be roan, a blending of red and white hairs in its coat, rather than either all red or all white.

During meiosis, or division of the reproductive (sperm and egg) cells, each pair of chromosomes splits, and one-half of each pair goes into one of the two new cells. Thus, in the case of eye color genes, one new reproductive cell will get the chromosome carrying the blue eye gene, while the other new reproductive cell will get the chromosome carrying the brown eye gene, and so on for each pair of chromosomes. If an organism has only one pair of chromosomes—called pair A, made up of chromosomes A_1 and A_2, and pair B, made up of chromosomes B_1 and B_2—each new reproductive cell will get one chromosome from each pair, and four different combinations are possible: A_1 and B_1; A_1 and B_2; A_2 and B_1; or A_2 and B_2. If the blue eye gene is on A_1, the brown eye gene on A_2, and the gene for curly hair on B_1, and the gene for straight hair on B_2, each of the above combinations will exert a different genetic effect on the offspring. This different grouping of chromosomes in the new reproductive cell as a result of meiotic cell division is known as *INDEPENDENT ASSORTMENT* and is one reason why variation occurs in the offspring. In the dog, with 39 pairs of chromosomes, the possibilites of variation through independent assortment are tremendous.

But variation does not end here. For example, if two dominant genes, such as the genes for brown eyes and dark hair, were on the same chromosome, all brown-eyed people would have dark hair. Yet in instances where such joined or *LINKED* genes do occur, the two characteristics do not always appear together in the same offspring. This is due to a process known as a *CROSS-OVER* or *RECOMBINATION*. Recombination is the mutual exchange of corresponding blocks of genes between the two chromosomes in a pair. That is, during cell division, the two chromosomes may exchange their tip sections or other corresponding segments. If the segments exchanged contain the eye color genes, the brown eye gene will be transferred from the chromosome carrying the dark hair gene to the chromosome carrying the light hair gene, and then brown eyes will occur with light hair, provided that the individual is homozygous for the recessive light hair gene.

Another important source of variation is *MUTATION*. In mutation, a gene becomes altered, such as by exposure to irradiation, and exerts a different effect than it did before. Most mutations are harmful to the organism, and some may result in death. Offspring carrying mutated genes and showing the effects of these mutations are known as *MUTANTS* or *SPORTS*. Mutation also means that instead of only two alleles for eye color, such as brown and blue, there may now be three or more (gray, black, etc.) creating a much larger source for possible variation in the offspring.

Further complications in the transmission and appearance of genetic traits are the phenomena known as *EPISTATIS* and *PLEIOTROPY*. Epistatis refers to a gene exerting influence on genes other than its own allele. In all-white red-eyed (albino) guinea pigs, for example, the gene controlling intensity of color is epistatic to any other color gene and prevents that gene from producing its effect. Thus, even if a gene for red spots were present in the cells of the guinea pig, the color intensity gene would prevent the red spots from appearing in the guinea pig's white coat. *Pleiotropy* refers to the fact that a single gene may control a number of characteristics. In the fruit fly, for example, the gene that controls eye color may also affect the structure of certain body parts and even the lifespan of the insect.

One special pair of chromosomes is known as the sex chromosomes. In man, dog, and other mammals, these chromosomes are of two types, designated as X and Y. Under normal conditions, a mammal carrying one X-type and one Y-type is a male. Females have two X chromosomes and can only contribute X chromosomes to the offspring, but the male can contribute either an X or a Y.

If the male's sperm carrying an X chromosome fertilizes the female's egg cell (X), the offspring (XX) will be a female; if a sperm carrying a Y chromosome fertilizes the egg (X), the offspring (XY) will be male. It is the male, therefore, that determines the sex of the offspring in mammals.

Traits controlled by genes present on the sex chromosome, and which appear in only one sex, are said to be *SEX LINKED*. If, for example, a rare recessive gene occurs on the X chromosome, it cannot exert its effect in the female because the dominant allele on the other X chromosomes will counteract it. In the male, however, there is no second X chromosome, and if the Y chromosome cannot offer any countereffect, the recessive character will appear. There are also *SEX-LIMITED* characteristics: these appear primarily or solely in one sex, but the genes for these traits are not carried on the sex chromosomes. Sex-limited traits appear when genes on other chromosomes exert their effect in the proper hormonal (male or female) environment. Sex-linked and sex-limited transmission is how a trait may skip a generation, by being passed from grandfather to grandson through a mother in which the trait, though present, does not show.

In dealing with the simplest form of heredity—one gene effecting one character—there is an expected ratio of the offspring displaying the character to those who do not display it, depending upon the genetic makeup of the parents. If a parent is homozygous for a character, such as blue eyes, it makes no difference which half of the chromosome pair enters the new reproductive cell, because each chromosome carries the gene for blue eyes. If a parent is heterozygous, however, one reproductive cell will receive the brown eye gene while the other will receive the blue eye gene. If both parents are homozygous for blue eyes, all the offspring will receive two blue eye genes, and all will have blue eyes. If a parent is homozygous for blue eyes, and the other parent is homozygous for brown eyes, all the offspring will be heterozygous, receiving one brown eye and one blue eye gene, and because brown is dominant, all will have brown eyes. If both parents are heterozygous, both the blue eye gene and the brown eye gene from one parent have an equal likelihood of ending up with either the blue eye or the brown eye gene from the other parent. This results in a ratio of two heterozygous offspring to the one homozygous for brown eyes and one homozygous for blue eyes, giving a total genetic, or genotypic, ratio of 2:1:1 or, as it is more commonly arranged, 1:2:1. As the two heterozygous as well as the homozygous brown eye offspring will have brown eyes, the ratio of brown eyes to blue eyes (or phenotypic ratio) will be 3:1.

If one parent is heterozygous and the other parent is homozygous for the recessive gene for blue eyes, but the other half of the offspring will be heterozygous and have brown eyes. (Here both the genotypic and phenotypic ratio is 1:1.)

If the homozygous parent, however, has the dominant gene (brown eyes), half of the offspring will be heterozygous and half will be homozygous, as before, but all will have brown eyes. By repeated determinations of these ratios in the offspring, geneticists are able to analyze the genetic makeup of the parents.

Before leaving heredity, it might be well to explain the difference between inbreeding, outcrossing, line breeding, and similar terms. Basically, there are only inbreeding and outbreeding. Inbreeding, however, according to its intensity, is usually divided into interbreeding proper and line breeding. Inbreeding proper is considered to be the mating of very closely related individuals, generally within the immediate family, but this is sometimes extended to include matings to first cousins and grandparents. Line breeding is the mating of more distantly related animals, that is, animals not immediately related to each other but having a common ancestor, such as the same grandsire or great-grandsire. Outbreeding is divided into outcrossing, which is the mating of dogs from different families within the same breed, and cross-breeding, which is mating purebred dogs from different breeds.

From the foregoing discussion of genetics, it should be realized that the theory of telegony, which states that the sire of one litter can influence future litters sired by other studs, is simply not true; it is possible, however, if several males mate with a female during a single estrus cycle, that the various puppies in the litter may have different sires (but not two sires for any one puppy). It should also be realized that blood does not really enter into the transmission of inheritance, although people commonly speak of "bloodlines," "pure-blooded," etc.

7. CARE OF THE MOTHER AND THE NEW FAMILY

PRENATAL CARE OF THE FEMALE

You can expect the puppies nine weeks from the day of breeding, although 58 days is as common as 63. During this time the female should receive normal care and exercise. If she is overweight, don't increase her food at first; excess weight at whelping time is not good. If she is on the thin side, build her up, giving her a morning meal of cereal and egg yolk. Consult your veterinarian as to increasing her vitamins and mineral supplement. During the last weeks the puppies grow enormously, and the mother will have little room for food and less appetite. Divide her meals into smaller portions and feed her more often. If she loses her appetite, tempt her with meat, liver, chicken, etc.

As she grows heavier, eliminate violent exercise and jumping. Do not eliminate exercise entirely, as walking is beneficial to the female in whelp, and mild exercise will maintain her muscle tone in preparation for the birth. Weigh your female after breeding and keep a record of her weight each week thereafter. Groom your bitch daily—some females have a slight discharge during gestation, more prevalent during the last two weeks, so wash the vulva with warm water daily. Usually, by the end of the fifth week you can notice a broadening across her loins, and her breasts become firmer. By the end of the sixth week your veterinarian can tell you whether or not she is pregnant.

PREPARATION OF WHELPING QUARTERS

Prepare a whelping box a few days before the puppies are due, and allow the mother to sleep there overnight or to spend some time in it during the day to become accustomed to it. Then she is less likely to try to have her pups under the front porch or in the middle of your bed. The box should have a wooden floor. Sides about a foot high will keep the puppies in but enable the mother to get out after she has fed them. If the weather is cold, the box should be raised about an inch off the floor.

You should place a guard rail in the whelping box to prevent the mother from rolling over onto the pups and smothering them. This guard is a strip of wood which will project out and above the floor of the box, keeping the bitch from pressing up against the sides of the box.

GUARD RAIL

SIDE BOARDS · ADDED LATER

STEP

ONE SIDE HINGED
FOR EASY CLEANING

WHELPING BOX

Layers of newspaper spread over the whole area will make excellent bedding and be absorbent enough to keep the surface warm and dry. They should be removed daily and replaced with another thick layer. An old quilt or washable blanket makes better footing for the nursing puppies than slippery newspaper during the first week, and is softer for the mother. The quilt should be secured firmly.

SUPPLIES TO HAVE ON HAND

As soon as you have the whelping box prepared, set up the nursery by collecting the various supplies you will need when the puppies arrive. You should have the following items on hand: a box lined with towels for the puppies, a heating pad or hot water bottle to keep the puppy box warm, a pile of clean terrycloth towels or washcloths to remove membranes and to dry puppies, a stack of folded newspapers, a roll of paper towels, vaseline, rubber gloves, soap, iodine, muzzle, cotton balls, a small pair of blunt scissors to cut umbilical cords (place scissors into an open bottle of alcohol so they keep freshly sterilized), a rectal thermometer, white thread, a flashlight in case the electricity goes off, a waste container, and a scale for weighing each puppy at birth.

It is necessary that the whelping room be warm and free from drafts, because puppies are delivered wet from the mother. Keep a little notebook and pencil handy so you can record the duration of the first labor and the time between the arrival of each puppy. If there is trouble in whelping, this is the information that the veterinarian will want. Keep his telephone number handy in case you have to call him in an emergency, and warn him to be prepared for an emergency, should you need him.

WHELPING

Be prepared for the actual whelping several days in advance. Usually the female will tear up papers, try to dig nests, refuse food, and generally act restless and nervous. These may be false alarms; the real test is her temperature, which will drop to below 100°F about twelve hours before whelping. Take her temperature rectally at a set time each day, starting about a week before she is due to whelp. After her temperature goes down, keep her constantly with you or put her in the whelping box and stay in the room with her. She will seem anxious and look to you for reassurance. During the birth, if neccesary, be prepared to remove the membranes covering the puppy's head if the mother fails to do this, for the puppy could smother otherwise.

The mother should start licking the puppy as soon as it is out of the sac, thus drying and stimulating it, but if she does not perform this task you can do it with a rough towel, instead. The afterbirth should follow the birth of each puppy, attached to the puppy by the umbilical cord. Watch to make sure that each is expelled, for retaining this material can cause infection. The mother probably will eat the afterbirth after biting the cord. One or two will not hurt her; they stimulate milk supply as well as labor for remaining puppies. Too many, however, can make her lose her appetite for the food she needs to feed her puppies and regain her strength, so remove the rest of them along with the soiled newspaper, and keep the box dry and clean to relieve her anxiety.

If a puppy does not start breathing, wrap him in a towel, hold him upside down with his head toward the ground, and shake him vigorously. If he still does not breathe, rub his ribs briskly; if this also fails, administer artificial respiration by compressing his ribs about twenty times per minute.

If the mother does not bite the cord, or bites it too close to the body, you should take over the job to prevent an umbilical hernia. Cut the cord a short distance from the body with your blunt scissors. Put a drop of iodine on the end of the cord; it will dry up and fall off in a few days.

The puppies should follow each other at regular intervals, but deliveries can be as short as five minutes or as long as two hours apart. A puppy may be presented backwards; if the mother does not seem to be in trouble, *do not interfere*. But if enough of the puppy is outside the birth canal, use a rough towel and help her by pulling gently on the puppy.

Pull only when she pushes. A rear-first, or breech birth can cause a puppy to strangle on its own umbilical cord, so don't let the mother struggle too long. Breech birth is quite common.

When you think all the puppies have been whelped, have your veterinarian examine the mother to determine if all the afterbirths have been expelled. He will probably give her an injection to be certain that the uterus is clean, a shot of calcium for prevention of eclampsia, and possibly an injection of penicillin to prevent infection.

CAESAREAN SECTION

Sometimes a Caesarean section is necessary, although very rarely. The operation of removing the pups by cutting into the abdomen and uterus of the bitch is generally safe; however, if the emergency Caesarean section follows a prolonged, exhausting and fruitless labor, the danger to the bitch is substantially increased.

Reasons for resorting to a Caesarean section include: 1. dystocia due to an abnormally large pup, 2. one presenting in such a way that it cannot get out, is blocking the passage and birth of its littermates or is threatening the life of its dam, 3. an abnormal pelvis in the bitch which does not allow passage of the pups (such as a previous pelvic fracture), 4. inertia, 5. long and arduous labor which exhausts the bitch to the point where weakness causes the uterine and abdominal contractions to stop.

Your bitch can be operated on without losing consciousness if your veterinarian selects to operate with a hypnotic and local anesthesia. The local anesthesia is injected, the incision made, and the pups taken from the semi-conscious bitch.

Gas anesthesia is the safest type of general anesthetic for delivering pups; if barbiturate anesthetics are used intravenously, the puppies may be quite effected by these drugs as they pass through the placental barrier.

Regardless of which method is used for the Caesarean section, the patient should be kept in a warm, clean bed after surgery until she recovers from the anesthesia. The pups should not be placed with the dam until she is once again alert. If the pups are also depressed from the anesthetic, artificial respiration may be required. It is imperative that the pups be kept dry and warm following the delivery.

Offer the puppies to their mother one at a time. After she licks a pup, help it to get settled on a teat and observe them carefully. Rarely, the bitch may not accept her puppies, but this may only be a temporary situation. Watch the mother when she goes out to do her duties; her sutures (stitches) should not be subjected to any undue strain. A binder may interfere with emptying several breasts, but aside from this she will behave in a normal manner. The stitches will be removed in about two weeks and she will be as good as new.

In the cases of both normal and Caesarean delivery the female's temperature should be checked twice daily for one week after delivery. A temperature of over 102°F should be reported to your veterinarian and his directions followed to the letter.

ECLAMPSIA

Eclampsia, or "milk fever," is caused by a lowered calcium content of the blood, due to the bitch's depleting her body's calcium reserves for the production of milk. It is a word that has been fearsome in the dog-breeding world for many years. If it occurs after whelping, the puppies and the mother are in severe danger. Help must be given immediately. The female stiffens her legs, has pale gums, and is likely to have minor convulsions. Puppies must be taken from her and calcium and dextrose administered to her intravenously. However, this is a rare thing and the symptoms so obvious, that assuredly the owner's first thought is that something is wrong and that the veterinarian is needed at once. With proper nutrition during gestation and lactation, a lack of calcium is not to be expected. The best preventive medicine is to see that the female is parasite free, in good condition, and properly cared for from the day she is mated.

HOW TO TAKE CARE OF A LARGE LITTER

The size of a litter varies greatly. If your bitch has a large litter she may have trouble feeding all of the puppies. You can help her by preparing an extra puppy box. Leave half the litter with the mother and the other half in a warm place, changing their places at two-hour intervals at first. Later you may change them less frequently, leaving them all together except during the day. Try supplementary feeding, too, as soon as their eyes are open, since at about two weeks they will lap from a dish.

RAISING THE PUPPIES

Hold each puppy to a breast as soon as he is dry, for a good meal without competition. Then he may join his littermates in the basket, out of his mother's way, while she is whelping. Keep a supply of evaporated milk on hand for emergencies, or later weaning. A formula of evaporated milk, corn syrup and a little water with egg yolk should be warmed and fed in a doll or baby bottle if necessary. A supplementary feeding often helps weak pups over the hump. Keep track of birth weights and take weekly readings so you will have an accurate record of the pups' growth and health.

This compartmentalized incubator demonstrates one method of caring for orphaned puppies. Orphaned pups need to be kept warm by artificial means since they do not have their mother to cuddle next to.

After the puppies have arrived, take the mother outside for a walk and drink, and then leave her to take care of them. She will probably not want to stay away more than a minute or two for the first few weeks. Be sure to keep water available at all times, and feed her milk or broth frequently, as she needs liquids to produce milk. To encourage her to eat, offer her the foods she likes best, until she asks to be fed without your tempting her. She will soon develop a ravenous appetite and should have at least two large meals a day, with dry food available in addition.

Prepare a warm place to put the puppies after they are born to keep them dry and help them to a good start in life. Cover an electric heating pad or hot-water bottle with flannel and put it in the bottom of a cardboard box. Set the box near the mother so that she can see her puppies. She will usually allow you to help, but don't take the puppies out of sight, and let her handle things if your interference seems to make her nervous.

Be sure that all of the puppies are getting enough to eat. If the mother sits or stands, instead of lying still to nurse, the probable cause is scratching from the puppies's nails. You can remedy this by clipping them, as you do hers. Manicure scissors will do for these tiny claws.

The puppies should normally be completely weaned at six weeks, although you start to feed them at three weeks. They will find it easier to lap semi-solid food. At four weeks they will eat four meals a day, and soon do without their mother entirely. Start them on mixed dog food, or leave it with them in a dish for self-feeding. Don't leave water with them all the time; at this age everything is to play with and they will use it as a wading pool. They can drink all they need if it is offered several times a day, after meals.

As the puppies grow up the mother will go into the pen only to nurse them, first sitting up and then standing. To dry her up completely, keep the mother away for longer periods, and then completely. The little milk left will be reabsorbed.

AIRING THE PUPPIES

The puppies may be put outside, unless it is too cold, as soon as their eyes are open. They will benefit from the sunlight and the vitamin D it provides. A rubber mat or newspapers underneath will protect them from cold or damp.

WORMING

You can expect a litter of pups to need at least one worming before they are ready to go to new homes, so take a stool sample to your veterinarian at about six weeks of age. Also, the litter should receive their first temporary shots, which are usually distemper-hepatitis-leptospirosis globulin. Today many kennels are advised by veterinarians to administer these preventative shots even earlier than six weeks, and in special cases they may begin right after birth. The puppy derives immunity from his mother's milk during the first twenty-four hours of his life; this immunity lasts for a varying length of time. Some mothers do not offer any immunity to their young at all. Therefore, in a kennel where the exposure rate is high, and many dogs come and go to shows, and disease may easily be brought to the premises, prophylactic treatment must start early. In the average home, where there is one female and one litter, six weeks is the proper time to start this treatment, and it must be repeated every one to two weeks until the puppies are old enough to have their permanent shots.

PUPPY SOCIALIZATION

Animal psychologists, research scientists and people who train dogs to work closely with people, such as trainers of seeing-eye dogs, have found that the first few weeks of a puppy's life is a critical time. The treatment a puppy receives during this stage determines whether he will become a mentally stable, trustworthy dog that likes people and is able to fit into their particular lifestyle. In general, the dog that is to be a reliable show dog or loving pet must be cuddled often, and experience pleasurable associations with people from a very early age. It is the duty of every creditable breeder to be willing to commit the amount of time necessary to socialize his puppies before he decides to breed his bitch. The behavior of his puppies, whether they are show prospects or pets, reflects on the breed and on his kennel name, two very good reasons for giving the puppies the kind of exposure to human companionship that will turn them into desirable adult dogs. This is not to deny heredity, but to stress the importance of human association in the early weeks of a puppy's life.

Some experts feel that the first three weeks of a puppy's life are completely taken up with nursing, sleeping and keeping warm snuggling with his littermates and dam, and that people-geared socialization should begin after these first three weeks. Others feel that it should begin right away, but that the form varies with the age. During the first weeks while the puppy is still gaining strength and weight and until his eyes are open, socialization should consist of simply holding the tiny pup, stroking its back and tummy for a few minutes and then putting it back with its mother. This should take place with each puppy, every day. As the puppy grows older, the time can be lengthened.

When the puppies are old enough to start eating solid foods, you can reinforce the pleasure contact by feeding them by hand. Basic training and developing receptivity to further training when they are older takes place at this point, so when you call them to you for the hand-held food, always use the same catch phrase. When the puppies are about a month old it's time to reinforce their sense of self-sufficiency and ease in new surroundings. This will also ease the transition to a new home. Remove the pups from their whelping box, which until now has circumscribed nearly their entire world, and take them to a different scene. The pup with the most adaptable nature is the one who will immediately move about and begin to explore this new setting. Puppies that are frightened and do not relax after a short time in this new environment should be put back with their mates until next time.

When they are six weeks old, puppies can be further disposed to training by putting a collar on them so they will get used to the feeling of it. Then put on the leash, not to take them for a walk, but just to let them run around in it so they get used to the idea. Later, more serious training can take place by the new owner with the puppy that is taking his place as a temperamentally sound, self-assured, friendly youngster in the world of his human companions.

8. GENERAL HEALTH CARE

WATCHING YOUR PUPPY'S HEALTH

First, don't be frightened by the number of diseases a dog can contract. The majority of dogs never get any of them. Don't become a dog-hypochondriac. All dogs have days when they feel lazy and want to lie around doing nothing. For the few diseases that you might be concerned about, remember that your veterinarian is your dog's best friend. When you first get your puppy, select a veterinarian whom you have faith in. He will get to know your dog and will be glad to have you consult him for advice. A dog needs little medical care, but that little is essential to his good health and well-being. He needs:

1. Proper diet at regular hours
2. Clean, roomy housing
3. Daily exercise
4. Companionship and love
5. Frequent grooming
6. Regular check-ups by your veterinarian

THE USEFUL THERMOMETER

Almost every serious ailment shows itself by an increase in the dog's body temperature. If your dog acts lifeless, looks dull-eyed, and gives the impression of illness, check his temperature by using a rectal thermometer. A stubby end rectal thermometer of either plastic or glass is best suited for this procedure. Although uncommon, there is always the hazard of possible breakage should he become excited during insertion. However, he is easily calmed if you soothe him when the routine is taking place. Hold the dog securely, and insert the thermometer, which you have lubricated with vaseline, and take a reading. The average normal temperature for your dog will be 101.5 °F. Excitement may raise the temperature slightly, but any rise of more than a few points is cause for alarm, and your vet should be consulted.

EMERGENCY FIRST AID

In general, a dog will heal his wounds by licking them. If he swallows anything harmful, chances are that he will throw it up. But it will probably make you feel better to help him if he is hurt, so treat his wounds as you would your own. Wash out the dirt and apply an antiseptic.

If you fear that your dog has swallowed poison, get him to the veterinarian's *at once*. In the meantime, try and locate the source of poisoning; if he has swallowed, for example, a cleaning fluid kept in your house, check the bottle label to see if inducing the dog to vomit is necessary. In some cases, inducing the dog to vomit can be very harmful, depending upon the type of poison swallowed. Amateur diagnosis is very dangerous, when you consider that time is so extremely important.

Accidents

Accidents, unfortunately, will happen so it is best to be prepared. If your dog gets hit by a car, keep him absolutely quiet, move him as little as possible and get veterinary treatment as soon as possible. It is unwise to give any stimulants such as brandy or other alcoholic liquids where there is visible external hemorrhage or the possibility of internal hemorrhaging. If your dog has cut his foot or leg badly, on glass or otherwise, bandage the wound as tightly as possible to stop the bleeding. A wad of cotton may serve as a pressure bandage, which will ordinarily stop the flow of blood. Gauze wrapped around the cotton will hold it in place. Usually, applying such pressure to a wound will sufficiently stop the blood flow; however, for severe bleeding, such as when an artery is cut, a tourniquet may be necessary. Apply a tourniquet between the injury and the heart if the bleeding is severe. To tighten the tourniquet, push a pencil through the bandage and twist it. Take your dog to a veterinarian immediately since a tourniquet should not be left in place any longer than fifteen minutes.

Blood coming from an artery is bright red in color and will spurt in unison with the heart beat. From a vein, it is dark red and continuous in flow.

Burns and Scalds

Any dog kept in the home runs the risk of being burned or scalded at one time or another. If your pet sustains a serious burn, call the vet immediately as shock quickly follows such a burn. The dog should be kept warm and quiet, wrapped in a blanket. If he still shows signs of being chilled, use a hot water bottle. Clean the burn gently, removing any foreign matter such as bits of lint, hair, grass or dirt. Act as quickly as possible. Prevent exposure to air by applying olive oil or another similar substance and cover with gauze, cotton and a loose bandage. To prevent the dog from interfering with the dressing, muzzle him and have someone stay with him until veterinary treatment is at hand.

If the burn or scald is a minor one clip hair away from the affected area and apply a paste of bicarbonate of soda and water. Apply it thickly to the burned area and try to keep the dog from licking it off.

Often the only way to adequately determine the best treatment for your dog is through microscopic analysis of a blood smear or tissue scraping so the veterinarian can diagnose the ailment exactly.

Snake Bite

If your dog is bitten by a poisonous snake, open up the wound with any available instrument that is sharp and clean. Squeeze the wound to cause a fair amount of blood to flow. This will wash the poison from the wound as much as possible. The dog should be taken to the veterinarian immediately so antitoxins can be administered. If the bite has been sustained on the leg, it is advisable to apply a tourniquet if at all possible to keep the poison from flowing further. Under no circumstances should snake bite from a poisonous snake, or its treatment, be taken lightly.

Stings

Many dogs enjoy trying to catch wasps and bees. When these insects are prevalent it is difficult to stop your pet from snapping at them. A sting frequently follows a successful catch and it often occurs inside the mouth, which can be very serious. The best remedy is to get him to a veterinarian as soon as possible, but there are some precautionary measures to follow in the meantime. If the dog has been lucky enough to only be caught on the outside of the face, try to extricate the stinger, then swab the point of entry with a solution of bicarbonate of soda. In the case of a wasp sting, use vinegar or some other acidic food stuff. A useful remedy for wasp stings is to rub the part with moistened tobacco, i.e., an unsmoked cigarette end that has been moistened.

IMPORTANCE OF INOCULATIONS

With the proper series of inoculations, your dog will be almost completely protected against disease. However, it occasionally happens that the shot does not take, and sometimes a different form of the virus appears against which your dog may not be protected.

Distemper

Probably the most virulent of all dog diseases is distemper. Young dogs are most susceptible to it, although it may affect dogs of all ages. The dog will lose his appetite, seem depressed, chilled, and run a fever. Often he will have a watery discharge from his eyes and nose. Unless treated promptly, the disease goes into advanced stages with infections of the lungs, intestines, and nervous system, and dogs that recover may be left with some impairment such as paralysis, convulsions, a twitch, or some other defect, usually spastic in nature. The best protection against this is very early inoculation with a series of permanent shots and a booster shot each year thereafter.

Hepatitis

Veterinarians report an increase in the spread of this viral disease in recent years, usually with younger dogs as the victims. The initial symptoms—drowsiness, vomiting, great thirst, loss of appetite, and a high temperature—closely resemble those of distemper. These symptoms are often accompanied by swellings of the head, neck, and abdomen. The disease strikes quickly; death may occur in just a few hours. Protection is afforded by injection with a vaccine recently developed.

Leptospirosis

This disease is carried by bacteria that live in stagnant or slow-moving water. It is carried by rats and dogs; infection is begun by the dog's licking substances contaminated by the urine or feces of infected animals. The symptoms are diarrhea and a yellowish-brownish discoloration of the jaws, tongue, and teeth, caused by an inflammation of the kidneys.

This disease can be cured if caught in time, but it is best to ward it off with a vaccine which your veterinarian can administer along with the distemper shots.

Rabies

This is an acute disease of the dog's central nervous system. It is spread by infectious saliva transmitted by the bite of an infected animal. Rabies is generally manifested in one of two classes of symptoms. The first is "furious rabies," in which the dog shows a period of melancholy or depression, then irritation, and finally paralysis. The first period lasts from a few hours to several days. During this time the dog is cross and will change his position often. He loses his appetite for food and begins to lick, bite and swallow foreign objects. During the irritative phase the dog is spasmodically wild and has impulses to run away. He acts in a fearless manner and runs at and bites everything in sight. If he is caged or confined he will fight at the bars, often breaking teeth or fracturing his jaw. His bark becomes a peculiar howl. In the final, or paralytic stage, the animal's lower jaw becomes paralyzed and hangs down; he walks with a stagger and saliva drips from his mouth. Within four to eight days after the onset of paralysis, the dog dies.

The second class of symptoms is referred to as "dumb rabies" and is characterized by the dog's walking in a bearlike manner, head down. The lower jaw is paralyzed and the dog is unable to bite. Outwardly, it may seem as though he had a bone caught in his throat.

Even if your pet should be bitten by a rabid dog or other animal, he probably can be saved if you get him to the veterinarian in time for a series of injections. However, after the symptoms have appeared no cure is possible. But remember that an annual rabies inoculation is almost certain protection against rabies. If you suspect that your dog has rabies, notify your local Health Department. A rabid dog is a danger to all who come near him.

HIP DYSPLASIA

This often crippling condition is more prevalent in large breeds than in small, but has occurred in almost every breed. The cause is not absolutely known though it is believed to be hereditary and as yet there is no known cure. The condition exists in varying degrees of severity. In general, hip dysplasia can be described as a poor fit between the two bones of the hip joint—the femur and the acetabulum—and is caused by a malformation of one or the other. Either the head of the femur is flattened causing it to slip out of the socket, or a shallowness of the acetabulum causes the femur to slip out. HD is usually graded according to severity and

Severely dysplastic hips, such as those pictured here, are incurable and hereditary. It is generally agreed that newborn puppies do not phenotypically exhibit the hip dysplasia trait and they begin life with properly fitted hips. The first signs of hip dysplasia become noticeable as unsteady movement in puppies at several months of age. Sometimes the gait of the puppy appears normal, but he tires very easily. The length of the stride is usually limited. The condition worsens with age, as the rim of the hip socket slowly wears down until there is no longer a proper fit between the femoral head of the hip bone and the hip socket. Since a predisposition for the disease is passed from parent to offspring, it is imperative that no dog exhibiting signs of hip dysplasia be used for breeding.

poorness of fit between the ball and socket, with the lowest grades being the best fit and the higher end of the scale denoting the worst cases.

HD causes stiffness in the hindlegs, considerable pain in the more severe cases and difficulty of movement. It generally manifests itself in puppyhood and can be noticed by the time the young dog is two months old. Severity can usually be determined by the age of six months. If HD is suspected, the dog should be x-rayed, and if afflicted it should not be used for breeding. Cases vary greatly, but severe pain may be more or less continuous in advanced cases. When this is true euthanasia is occasionally recommended, though medication is available to control the pain and allow the dog to move with more ease. Rigorous exercise is not recommended since it only increases the rate at which the bone surfaces wear away.

COUGHS, COLDS, BRONCHITIS, PNEUMONIA

Respiratory diseases may affect the dog because he is forced to live under man-made conditions rather than in his natural environment. Being subjected to cold or a draft after a bath, sleeping near an air conditioner or in the path of a fan or near a radiator can cause respiratory ailments. The symptoms are similar to those in humans. The germs of these diseases, however, are different and do not affect both dogs and humans, so they cannot be infected by each other. Treatment is much the same as for a child with the same type of illness. Keep the dog warm, quiet, and well fed. Your veterinarian has antibiotics and other remedies to help the dog recover.

DIABETES MELLITUS (Sugar Diabetes)

This is a disease wherein the sugar balance of the body is disturbed because of insufficient production of the hormone insulin. The pancreas secretes insulin which regulates carbohydrate/sugar usage. When the insulin-producing cells are damaged, the condition arises. It is marked by an increase in the blood sugar level and an excessive amount of sugar is excreted in the urine.

Symptoms of the condition are great thirst, increased urination and loss of weight while the appetite and food consumption increases. The signs vary in severity. If overlooked, emaciation and collapse rapidly occur. The dog can go into a diabetic coma and die.

Treatment is the same as for human diabetes, utilizing dietary regulation and insulin injections if necessary. The diet should be one of very low fat, with a low percentage of carbohydrate and a higher pecentage of protein. The insulin dose must be adjusted as indicated by urine tests which your veterinarian can teach you to administer at home. The test makes use of chemically treated sticks, pale yellow in color, which turn to various shades of green when dipped in urine. The darker the shade, the more serious the condition.

INTERNAL PARASITES

There are four common internal parasites that may infect your dog. These are roundworms, hookworms, whipworms, and tapeworms. The first three can be diagnosed by laboratory examination; the presence of tapeworms is determined by seeing segments in the stool or attached to the hair around the tail. Do not under any circumstances attempt to worm your dog without the advice of your veterinarian. After first determining what type of worm or worms are present, he will advise you of the best method of treatment.

A dog or puppy in good physical condition is less susceptible to worm infestation than a weak dog. Proper sanitation and a nutritious diet help in preventing worms. One of the best preventative measures is to always have clean, dry bedding for your dog. This will diminish the possibility of reinfection due to flea or tick bites.

Heartworms

Heartworm infestation in dogs is passed by mosquitoes and can be a life threatening problem. Dogs with the disease tire easily, have difficulty breathing, cough and may lose weight despite a hearty appetite. If caught in the early stages, the disease can be effectively treated; however, the administration of daily preventative medicine throughout the spring, summer and fall months is strongly advised. Your veterinarian must first take

Pictured is the heart of a dog showing a heavy infestation of heartworms. Mosquitoes carry the offspring of the adult worms which are implanted into a dog's bloodstream when the dog is bitten. The worm offspring travel to the heart where they do their damage as they develop into adult worms.

U.S.D.A.

Eggs of certain parasites commonly seen in dogs.

Round Worm
(Ascarid)

Tapeworm

Hookworm

Whipworm

The presence of worms in your dog's system can manifest itself in outward signs such as a general deterioration, loss of weight, dulling of coat, diarrhea and vomiting. *Roundworm* larvae penetrate the intestinal lining, where they enter the bloodstream and are carried to the lungs. This worm affects mostly puppies, in whom it can cause lung damage and intestinal blockage. There are many species of *tapeworm* that can infest your dog. The important factor in breaking the life cycle of the tapeworm is the elimination of the parasitic host on which the worm thrives. Fleas are perhaps the most common host, so ridding your dog of them is a step toward eliminating the possibility of tapeworm infection. If present in massive quantities, *hookworms*, which remove blood from the dog, may cause circulatory collapse and ultimate death. *Whipworms* may cause weight loss, vomiting, diarrhea and secondary anemia in an affected dog.

a blood sample from your dog to test for the presence of the disease, and if the dog is heartworm-free, pills or liquid medicine can be prescribed that will protect against any infestation.

It was formerly believed that heartworms occured only in warmer climates, but it is now known that they may occur anywhere that they can be carried by any of several species of mosquitoes.

Adult worms are found in the right side of the heart, the vena cavae and the pulmonary artery. There the eggs develop and are released as microfilariae. The microfilariae circulate in the blood of the dog until a mosquito ingests them, starting the larval growth cycle. Being carried by the various mosquito species induces the third-stage larval development. The third-stage larvae are re-deposited during a subsequent feeding by the mosquito and proceed to grow.

Microfilariae remain inactive while in the blood of the dog in which they were originally deposited by the female. It is only after they have been ingested by a subsequent mosquito and redeposited in another host that they begin to develop. These larvae lodge in subcutaneous tissue or muscle where they stay about three months; at between three and four months they migrate to the heart. Three to four months later the adult worm begins producing microfilariae.

Adult worms are creamy white in color. The female grows to 11 or 12 inches in length, the male, to six or seven inches. The sexes are distinquished by length since both are about the diameter of the lead in a mechanical pencil. Each mature female worm is capable of producing 30,000 microfilariae each day. A hundred adult females can account for about two billion microfilariae in the body of a dog since microfilariae live up to two years.

Apparently canines of all ages are susceptible to heartworm infestation, but they must have been exposed to mosquitoes in order to have acquired the third-stage infective larvae. Heartworm infection increases markedly as the dog matures. If left undetected, it will erode the heart.

A microscopic search for microfilariae is necessary to prove that adult worms are present. Because of the large number and size of the worms, treatment must be careful and slow to minimize damage to the circulatory system.

SKIN AILMENTS

Any persistent scratching may indicate an irritation. Whenever you groom your dog, look for the reddish spots that may indicate eczema, mange, or fungal infection. Rather than treating your dog yourself, take him to the veterinarian, as some of the conditions may be difficult to eradicate and can cause permanent damage to his coat.

Two of the most common external parasites are the tick (left) and the flea (right). Along with the general discomfort and irritation that they bring to your dog, these parasites can infest him with worms and disease. The flea is a carrier of tapeworm, and may act as an intermediate host for heartworm. The tick can cause dermatitis and anemia in your dog, and may also be a carrier of Rocky Mountain spotted fever and canine babesiasis, a blood infection.

External Parasites

The dog that is groomed regularly and provided with clean sleeping quarters should not be troubled by fleas, ticks, or lice. If the dog should become infested with any of these parasites, he should be treated with medicated dip bath or the new oral medications that are presently available.

Mange

There are two types of mange, sarcoptic and follicular, both of which are caused by a parasite. The former is by far the more common, and results in an intense irritation, causing violent scratching. Close examination will reveal small red spots which become filled with pus. This is a highly contagious condition, and any dog showing signs of the disease should be isolated. Consult your veterinarian for the proper treatment procedures. Follicular mange is very much harder to cure, but fortunately, it is much rarer and less contagious. This disease will manifest itself as bare patches appearing on the skin, which becomes thickened and leathery. A complete cure from this condition is only rarely effected.

Eczema

This disease occurs most often in the summer months and affects the dog down the back, especially just above the root of the tail. It should not be confused with mange, as it is not caused by a parasite. One of the principle causes of eczema is improper nutrition, which makes the dog susceptible to disease. Hot, humid weather predisposes the growth of bacteria, which can invade a susceptible dog and thereby cause skin irritations and lesions. It is imperative that the dog gets relief from the itching that is symptomatic of the disease as this self-mutilation by scratching will only help to spread the inflammation. Antibiotics may be necessary if a bacterial infection is, indeed, present. The dog must be thoroughly ridded of fleas to avoid any recurrance of the scratching that can spread the disease.

Moist eczema, commonly referred to as "hot spots," is a rapidly appearing skin disease that produces a moist infection. Spots appear very suddenly and may spread rapidly in a few hours, infecting several parts of the body. These lesions are generally bacterially infected and are extremely itchy, which will cause the dog to scratch frantically and further damage the afflicted areas. Vomiting, fever and an enlargement of the lymph nodes may occur. The infected areas must be clipped to the skin and thoroughly cleaned. Your veterinarian will prescribe an anti-inflammatory drug and antibiotics, as well as a soothing emollient to relieve itching.

EYES, EARS, TEETH AND NAILS

If your dog is to remain in good health, you must be aware of the need for periodic "examinations" in which you routinely inspect him for unusual signs of irritation or infection. In most cases, the tell-tale warning signals are any unusual swelling, discharge or redness that may appear, especially after an injury.

The eyes, because of their sensitivity, are prone to injury and infection. Dogs that spend a great deal of time outdoors in heavily wooded areas may return from an exercise excursion with watery eyes, the result of brambles and high weeds scratching them. The eyes may also be irritated by dirt and other foreign matter.

Should your dog's eyes appear red and watery, a mild solution can be mixed at home for a soothing washing. Your veterinarian will be able to tell you what percentage of boric acid, salt, or other medicinal compound to mix with water.

You must monitor your dog's eyes after such a solution is administered; if the irritation persists, or if there is a significant discharge, immediate veterinary attention is warranted.

Your dog's ears, like his eyes, are extremely sensitive and can also be prone to infection, should wax and/or dirt be allowed to build up. Ear irritants may be present in the form of mites, soap or water, or foreign par-

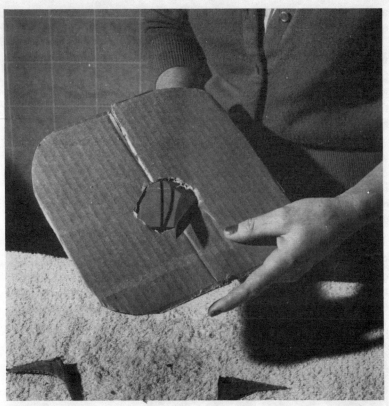

The Elizabethan collar is designed to keep your dog from scratching the area about his head and ears when a wound or sutures there advise against scratching. While they can be purchased ready-made, they can also be easily made at home from a piece of cardboard box. Be sure the hole is large enough so that it does not constrict the dog's breathing or swallowing.

ticles which the dog has come into contact with while romping through a wooded area. If your dog's ears are bothering him, you will know it—he will scratch and paw them, shake his head, and the ears will show a foul-smelling dark secretion. This pasty secretion usually signals the onset of *otorrhea*, or ear canker, and at this stage proper veterinary care is essential if the dog's hearing is not to be permanently impaired. In the advanced stages of ear canker, tissue builds up within the ear, and the ear canal becomes blocked off, thus eliminating the hearing abilities of that ear.

If this is to be prevented, you should wash your dog's ears as they require it, with a very dilute solution of hydrogen peroxide and water, or an antibacterial ointment, as your vet suggests. In any case, the ears, because of their delicacy, are to be washed gently, with a soft cloth or cotton.

The good health of your pet's teeth can be maintained by his regular use of a chew product such as Nylabone® or Nylaball®, which serves to clean the teeth of tartar accumulation and massage and stimulate the gums. With puppies, a chew product helps to relieve the discomfort of the teething stage, and of course prevents the pup's chewing of your furniture and slippers!

A periodic inspection of your dog's mouth will alert you to any problem he might have that would require a trip to the veterinarian's office. Any signs of tooth or gum sensitivity, redness or swelling, signal the need for professional treatment. Also, it is best to have your pet's teeth scraped once or twice a year, at the time that he goes to the vet's for his general physical check-up. This simple procedure removes any excess tartar that

Badly decayed teeth can cause abscesses of mouth tissues and gums, and even bone deterioration in extreme cases. Pain caused by such a condition can discourage your dog from eating even though he is hungry, resulting in possible malnutrition or even starvation. Your vet should be consulted if any listlessness or change in eating habits is noticed.

Dog nail clippers are designed to trim nails quickly and easily with a minimum of scuffling between you and your dog. While other general purpose instruments can be used, there is a greater chance with these of cutting too far down on the nail and hitting the vein, resulting in a painful experience for your dog.

has accumulated on his teeth that could cause degeneration of tooth enamel, if left to build up.

If you live in a city and walk your dog regularly on pavement, chances are that his nails are kept trimmed from the "wear and tear" they receive from the sidewalks. However, if your dog gets all of his exercise in your yard, or if his nails simply grow rather quickly, it will occasionally be necessary for you to clip his nails. It is best for you to have your veterinarian show you the proper way to perform the nail clipping at first. Special care must always be taken to avoid cutting too far and reaching the "quick." If you cut into the quick of the nail, it will bleed, so it is easy to see why an expert must show you the proper procedure. A nail clipper designed especially for dogs can be purchased at any pet shop.

CARE OF THE AGED DOG

With the increased knowledge and care available, there is no reason why your dog should not live to a good old age. As the years go by he may need a little additional care. Remember that an excessively fat dog is not healthy, particularly as he grows older, so limit the older dog's food accordingly. He needs exercise as much as ever, although his heart cannot bear the strain of sudden and violent exertion. Failing eyesight or hearing means lessened awareness of dangers, so you must protect him more than ever.

Should you decide at this time to get a puppy, to avoid being without a dog when your old friend is no longer with you, be very careful how you introduce the puppy. He naturally will be playful and will expect the older dog to respond to his advances. Sometimes the old dog will get a new lease on life from a new puppy, but he may be consumed with jealousy. Do not give the newcomer the attention that formerly was exclusively the older dog's. Feed them apart, and show your old friend that you still love him the most; the puppy, not being accustomed to individual attention, will not mind sharing your love.

TATTOOING

Tattooing is an increasingly popular method of identifying your dog that has met with growing success in assuring the safe return of lost or stolen dogs. Several registries exist that will record a dog's tattoo number along with his owner's name, address and telephone number. Two types of tattoo numbers can be assigned. In the case of mixed breed dogs, the owner's social security number is generally used; in the case of pedigreed dogs, the dog's AKC registration number is used. These two numbers are the most common means of identification. The groin or inside of the ear is the usual spot for the tattoo mark, though cases have been cited in which a dog's ear was cut off to eliminate the possibility of catching the dognappers.

For a minor fee, your veterinarian can do the simple, painless job that may insure the return of a beloved pet or show dog. Such return would be reward enough for the few minutes it takes to have this simple procedure done. Since a puppy grows very rapidly, it is best not to have him tattooed until he is at least four months old to avoid any possible smearing of the tattoo ink. There is almost no danger of infection if the job is done properly and exhibitors run no risk of having the show dog's career impaired by the tattoo mark since the AKC has ruled that no judge may disqualify or penalize a dog because of a tattoo.

Your local kennel club will be able to supply the name of a registry in your area.

9. DOG SHOW COMPETITION

There is no greater pleasure for the owner than showing a beautiful dog perfectly groomed and trained for the show ring. Whether he wins or not, it is gratifying to show a dog in superb condition, one that is a credit to your training and care. A great deal of preparation, both for you and your dog, is needed before the day that you do any serious winning. Showing is not as easy as it looks, even if you have a magnificent dog. He must be presented to the judge so that all of his good points are shown to advantage. This requires practice in gaiting, daily grooming from puppyhood, and the proper diet to make him sound in body.

When you buy your puppy you probably will think he is the best in the country and possibly in the world, but before you enter the highly competitive world of dog shows, get an unbiased expert opinion. Visit a few dog shows as a spectator and make mental notes of what is required of the handlers and dogs. Watch how the experienced handlers manage their dogs to bring out their best points.

HOW TO SELECT A SHOW DOG

If you are planning to show your dog, it is best not to buy a puppy any younger than four or six months of age. Since it is difficult at best to predict what a puppy will look like at maturity, you cannot rely wholly on its appearance while it is only six or eight weeks old. By doing a certain amount of homework before purchasing your show dog, you can be assured to an extent that you will end up with a show quality dog that will hold its own in the show rings. Before going out to buy, read some good books on your breed. Consult a reputable book of standards for the breed to get an idea of what the dog should look like as an adult. Remember that no individual dog ever completely achieves the standard, but knowing the important conformational points of the breed will help to illustrate what you are aiming for in your show dog. Attending dog shows and talking with veterans who have been in the dog game for a while will give you valuable information to use when choosing your own show prospect.

One of the best assurances you can get in a field where there are no real guarantees is to search out well-known breeders who are known to have successfully bred show winners through several generations. Ask to look at the pedigree of any puppy you are considering buying, noting whether there are numerous top-quality dogs in the ancestry. Have the sire and

When you purchase your puppy, the breeder can supply you with a pedigree for him. A puppy of champion bloodlines is often of superior quality.

dam of the litter you are interested in been bred before, and if so, what was the overall quality of their previous offspring? If they have produced consistently good dogs through several of the same pairings, your chances of getting a good specimen are fairly high. If the stud or bitch, or both, are unproven in previous litters, the probability of attaining top quality in the puppies is less likely.

In general, the rule of thumb to follow is to go by the expertise of the breeder. A reputable breeder will sell you the best dog possible if you make it clear to him that the dog will definitely be used for a show career. The show contender you purchase not only represents you as its owner, but also reflects the quality of the kennel of the breeder. The reputation of both exhibitor and breeder is made by the quality of the dogs they present, so careful selection of a show dog is essential to all involved.

TYPES OF DOG SHOWS

There are various types of dog shows. The American Kennel Club sanctioned matches are shows at which purebred dogs may compete, but not for championship points. These are excellent for you to enter to accustom you and your dog to showing. If your dog places in a few match shows, then you might seriously consider entering the big-time shows. An American Kennel Club all-breed show is one at which purebred dogs compete for championship points. An American Kennel Club specialty show is for one breed only. It may be held in conjunction with an all-breed show (by designating the classes at that show as its specialty show) or it may be held entirely apart. Obedience trials are different in that in them the dog is judged according to his obedience and ability to perform, not by his conformation to the breed standard.

There are two types of championship conformation shows: *benched* and *unbenched*. At a benched show your dog must be on his appointed bench during the advertised hours of the show's duration. He may be removed from the bench only to be taken to the exercise pen or to be groomed (an hour before the showing) in an area designated for handlers to set up their crates and grooming tables. At an unbenched show your car may serve as a bench for your dog.

To become a champion your dog must win fifteen points in competition with other dogs; a portion of the fifteen points must be awarded as major point wins (three to five points) under different judges.

This scene from a large indoor show captures the exciting moment when the group winners go before the judge for the Best In Show competition.

HOW TO ENTER

If your dog is purebred and registered with the AKC—or eligible for registration—you may enter him in the appropriate show class for which his age, sex, and previous show record qualify him. You will find coming shows listed in the different dog magazines or at your petshop. Write to the secretary of the show, asking for the premium list. When you receive the entry form, fill it in carefully and send it back with the required entry fee. Then, before the show, you should receive your exhibitor's pass, which will admit you and your dog to the show. Here are the five official show classes:

PUPPY CLASS: Open to dogs at least six months and not more than twelve months of age. Limited to dogs whelped in the United States and Canada.

NOVICE CLASS: Open to dogs six months of age or older that have never won a first prize in any class other than puppy class, and less than three first prizes in the novice class itself. Limited to dogs whelped in the United States or Canada.

BRED BY EXHIBITOR CLASS: Open to all dogs, except cham-

To transport your dog long distances, crates should be used that have been made especially for that purpose. They are designed to give your dog optimum ventilation and comfort, while still assuring his maximum safety and protection.

Your pet store carries a large number of pet feeding and watering bowls, in sizes suitable for any size dog. While at a show, be sure to supply your dog with a light meal and some fresh water to keep him comfortable.

pions, six months of age or over which are exhibited by the same person, or his immediate family, or kennel that was the recognized breeder on the records of the American Kennel Club.

AMERICAN-BRED CLASS: Open to dogs that are not champions, six months of age or over, whelped in the United states after a mating which took place in the United States.

OPEN CLASS: Open to dogs six months of age or over, with no exceptions.

In addition there are local classes, the Specials Only class, and brace and team entries.

For full information on dog shows, read the book *How to Show Your Own Dog,* by Virginia Tuck Nichols. (T.F.H.)

JUNIOR SHOWMANSHIP

If you have considered that you and your dog are going to go the show route, you might consider having your youngster show the dog in the ring. If your child has an especially good relationship with his pet, or if he has trained the dog himself, as many children do, then Junior Showmanship might be a good learning experience.

Junior Showmanship is competition among children of different age groups, handling dogs owned by their immediate families. The age divisions are: Novice A, for 10 to 12 year olds; Novice B, for those boys and girls from 13 to 16 (entrants in these two classes must have one or no prior Junior Showmanship wins); Open A for those 10 to 12 years of age; Open B for those 13 to 16 (these entrants must have earned two or more Junior Showmanship awards).

Children involved in JS have the wonderful opportunity to feel a sense of achievement and victory, should they walk away with the ribbons after a show. Even still, winning is not the most important factor here: the pride and responsibility the youngster feels at having reached the ring is surely worth the effort and discipline required to enter showmanship competition.

For more information on JS, and to obtain a rules and regulations booklet, you can contact the American Kennel Club in New York.

ADVANCED PREPARATION

Before you go to a show your dog should be trained to gait at a trot beside you, with head up and in a straight line. In the ring you will have to gait your dog around the edge with other dogs and then individually up and down the center runner. In addition the dog must stand for ex-

If yours is intended to be a show dog, you will want to be prepared with all the tools and equipment necessary for the meticulous grooming of a show dog. Several different types of combs, brushes, clippers and coat grooming products can be obtained from the local pet store.

Be sure to take along a comfortable carrier for your dog if he is to be confined, or benched, during the show's duration.

amination by the judge, who will look at him closely and feel his head and body structure. He should be taught to stand squarely, hind feet slightly back, head up on the alert. Showing requires practice training sessions in advance. Get a friend to act as judge and set the dog up and "show" him a few minutes every day.

Sometime before the show, give your dog a bath so he will look his best. Get together all the things you will need to take to the show. You will want to take a water dish and a bottle of water for your dog (so he won't be affected by a change in drinking water). Take your show lead, bench chain (if it is a benched show), combs and brush, and the identification ticket sent by the show superintendent, noting the time you must be there and the place where the show will be held, as well as the time of judging.

THE DAY OF THE SHOW

Don't feed your dog the morning of the show, or give him at most a light meal. He will be more comfortable in the car on the way, and will show more enthusiastically. When you arrive at the show grounds, find out where he is to be benched and settle him there. Your bench or stall

Conformation to the ideal standard for the breed will be recognized in show dogs by the awarding of ribbons and trophies. Dog show entrants can win on several different levels, with the most significant and exciting award being Best In Show honors.

number is on your identification ticket, and the breed name will be on placards fastened to the ends of the row of benches. Once you have your dog securely fastened to his stall by a bench chain (use a bench crate instead of a chain if you prefer), locate the ring where your dog will be judged (the number and time of showing will be on the program of judging which came with your ticket). After this you may want to take your dog to the exercise ring to relieve himself, and give him a small drink of water. Your dog will have been groomed before the show, but give him a final brushing just before going into the show ring. When your breed judging is called, it is your responsibility to be at the ringside ready to go in. The steward will give you an armband which has on it the number of your dog.

Then, as you step into the ring, try to keep your knees from knocking! Concentrate on your dog and before you realize it you'll be out again, perhaps back with the winners of each class for more judging and finally, with luck, it will be over and you'll have a ribbon and trophy—and, of course, the most wonderful dog in the world!

10. BUILDING A KENNEL AND EXERCISE RUNS

DRAWING UP PLANS

Whether you have one dog or many, the time may come when you decide that an outdoor kennel and runs will best satisfy your dog's exercise and housing needs. Properly built and maintained, a kennel offers your dog the comfort of dry living quarters, adequate ventilation and sunlight, and the availability of regular exercise.

Before you begin to draw up plans for kennel construction, check with your town's municipal offices to see if a building permit is required and which, if any, regulations of the building code you must adhere to. The permit, if required, must be obtained before any construction is begun. Building a kennel is not a small undertaking, so pre-planning on all fronts will prevent unexpected snags from cropping up, causing time delays and inconveniences.

One of the first decisions to make concerns the choice between building the kennel yourself as a sort of family project, or hiring a general contractor to do the work. If you decide on the latter, details of financing, building plans and blueprints to suit your needs should be worked out before contractual agreements are signed. For the plans on actual construction, including a concrete foundation, framework and overall structure, you should consult an architect who will, for a fee, draw up a set of blueprints for you or a contractor to follow. Have the architect see your land, and detail clearly to him each specific feature you want designed into the building. In this way you will enable him to set down a precise set of blueprints, meeting your specifications.

LAND AND SPACE REQUIREMENTS

To build an average size kennel, you must have a significant parcel of land to set aside for this purpose. The location of the building site should provide adequate sunlight and shade for warmth and coolness throughout the seasons. The soil should be of a high gravel content as a gravel soil provides good drainage. By comparison, a sandy soil, though its surface dries quickly, retains dampness and residual dirt just beneath the surface. It is also a favorite breeding place of fleas and similar pests.

Drainage is a prime consideration, not only to let natural ground water run off, but also to let the water drain off from the frequent hosings a kennel must be given to ensure cleanliness and prevent growth of disease-producing germs. A kennel should be trenched for drainage much the way a soldier trenches around his tent. One continuous drainage ditch approximately eight inches wide should be dug around all sides of the kennel, no further than a foot away from the kennel walls. It should be dug to a depth of four inches to start with, sloping an additional inch for every three yards of land. With ditches extending from at least two front corners of the building down to this surrounding ditch, water will run away from the building to the lowest point of land, preventing moisture build-up or preventing the water to lay near the kennel building itself. The drainage system can be sophisticated further, the ditch tiled, for instance, and eventually connecting with or running to a storm drain. Whatever else is devised, drainage should definitely figure into your building plans.

BUILDING MATERIALS

The building materials you use are of great importance. Not only must they be of good quality but they must be of a type that will protect the dog from the elements. For example, sheet metal, a conductor of both heat and cold, should never be used for the outside walls or ceilings. It becomes extremely hot in the sun and will retain heat in the kennel, making a potentially dangerous and certainly uncomfortable situation for the dogs. Outside walls should ideally be constructed from lumber, bricks or cinder blocks. The walls must be insulated with a substance that will serve equally well in all seasons, protecting your dogs from the heat and the cold.

Interior walls can be constructed of wood, plywood or plaster board. Plywood has the advantage of being extremely durable; however, plywood is quite expensive and can give way to splintering should the dogs scratch at it. Plaster board, also commonly known as sheet rock, is inexpensive and relatively durable. Plaster board does not, however, stand up well to moisture, but more than compensates for this drawback by being very resistant to insect and rodent infestation.

The above plans detail the probable steps involved in the construction of a rather large kennel, suited for up to a dozen dogs. At first, most dog owners have only one or two dogs that they want to provide for. If this is the case, a large dog house, modified somewhat, will aptly serve until such time that a larger kennel is needed.

THE SINGLE DOG HOUSE

While a dog will be contented with less living space than his master is accustomed to, his own house should be large enough to allow for free space around and above him when he stands up in the enclosure. The size of the dog house depends, of course, on the size of the dog.

Using materials purchased from any lumber store, you can build a dog house yourself. When constructing the house, take care to finish it off well, leaving no nails or wood splinters protruding from the wood which could injure the dog.

If you wish to move your pet into a new, ready-to-go home, finished dog houses can be purchased in varying styles and price ranges. Your pet shop may have some houses in stock; if not, the owner can probably suggest an outlet where one would be available. The yellow pages of your phone directory may also be useful in locating an establishment that carries dog houses, either constructed or in kits. Some of the latest styles available are quite pleasing to the eye, such as the house constructed out of unstripped logs, designed to give your dog his own little log cabin! If you check various outlets you will find that dog houses range in design from the simple to the elaborate.

CARE OF THE DOG HOUSE

To prevent dampness and to retain heat in the dog house, it should not be placed directly on the ground, but elevated at least several inches. A 2" x 4" beam placed under two opposing sides of the house, with the 4" side lying flat on the ground, should allow for proper ventilation beneath the structure. However, in winter months you will want to close off this space to prevent drafts. In this case, boards can easily and quickly be nailed between the 2" x 4"'s already in place to cover the exposed openings. Keeping the dog house a proper distance from the ground also serves to prevent the possibility of water damage, which will cause the wood to warp and eventually decay. Infestation of the wood by insects can be prevented by keeping the primary wood of the house from contact with the dirt below.

Whether kept in the yard or in the garage, the single dog house has the advantage of being able to be moved from spot to spot. Moving the dog house will be necessary occasionally for such reasons as cleaning, moving into or out of direct sunlight or shade, etc. This is an advantage when you consider that in the cold winter months your dog may very much appreciate having his house placed in direct sunlight! In cold weather the dog house can be positioned with the entranceway facing east or south, to receive full sunlight.

If a shifting of position is all that is needed, a strong friend or two should be able to help relocate the house. However, if the move is for a considerable distance and your dog house is quite heavy, a moving dolly may be necessary.

1

2

(1) An adorable portrait: young littermates inquisitively peering out from their litter box. (2) A charming head study depicting the alertness of the breed. (3) Note the characteristic wrinkled skin of the legs on the specimen in the foreground.

3

The best type of roof for a dog house is a flat or sloping one which can be easily removed or opened at a hinge for cleaning, or to provide the dog with air and sunlight in the warmer months. A sloping roof does not allow excessive rain or snow to accumulate on the top and pose the possible hazard of having the roof collapse under the weight. When constructing the roof, or when purchasing the dog house, remember that it must be properly insulated from the elements. The most efficient form of all-weather protection is tarred roofing paper, covered by good shingles.

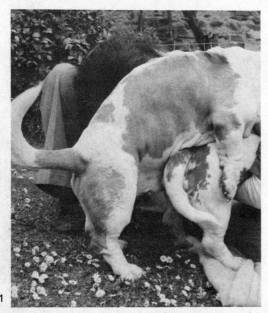

(1) During the mating ritual, the male mounts the bitch and begins exploratory thrusts toward penetration. (2) Once he has penetrated her, and a tie has taken place, the two rest side by side or tail to tail, until the swelling at the base of the male's penis subsides, usually from 15 minutes through about 45, and the two can separate.

1

2

11. COAT VARIETIES

The Basset Hound that we see today in conformation shows, tracking trials and in the home as a family pet is a smooth coated dog of true "hound color"—black, tan and white—distributed over the body in no particular pattern. However, there is another type of Basset besides the smooth coated, that we seldom see or hear mention of, but which enjoys even until this day a large amount of popularity in France—the rough-coated Basset, or "Basset Griffon."

The need for a rough coated Basset Hound was of primary concern to the hunters of the 1800's who went to the field in very rough terrain. The areas of Brittany, in the northwest of France, where Bassets were bred, were marked by jagged rocks and thorny underbrush, and as such required a hunting dog whose coat afforded some protection from the harsh environment. Thus, one of the strains developed by the Count le Couteulx de Cantelue, known as the *Fino de Paris* type, sported a thick crimped coat, with feathering about the body. When the Count went about his famous breeding work, this description was set down on the thick coated Basset: Coat: thick, strong, sometimes crimped, coarse, and feathered.

INFLUENCE OF ENVIRONMENT AND FUNCTION ON COAT

As with all dogs whose original purpose was as a worker for man, two things influenced the type, or physical appearance: the dogs' function, and the environment in which they lived. As an example, those dogs who were bred as draught dogs in mountainous terrain, such as the Bernese Mountain Dog of the Swiss Alps, adapted long, thick coats as protection against the harsh, bitter climate. The Basenji, a hound originally found as a dog of the pharoahs in ancient Egypt, but predominant now in Central Africa, where it is a dog of hunting expertise, developed a short coat as a result of the tropical climes in which it has thrived. As well, the type of prey it stalks in its native Africa, large reed rats among them, call for an exceptionally quiet, stealthy dog, and, as the Basenji is "barkless," he is well suited for this type of work.

And so it was with the Basset Hound, molded and "revised," if you will, for a specific purpose and for a specific environment. Originally, St. Hubert, living in a forest area where the landscape was made up of grassy expanses and woods, worked towards a specimen who would be suited to working its way with ease through the fields with a short smooth coat that

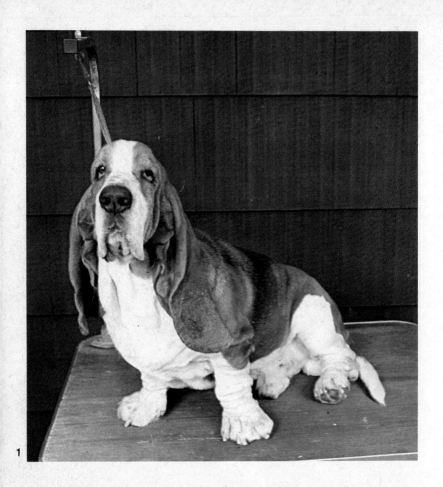

1

The Basset Hound is a dog requiring relatively little grooming; the little grooming that your pet will need can be effected easily and quickly several times a week. Before you begin any grooming, however, train your pup to tolerate the procedure and the grooming table itself. In (1), we see a grooming table complete with restraining collar, or "noose" as it is known, comfortably keeping the Basset in place. (2) shows the Basset being brushed. A natural bristle brush is a good choice because it is gentler on the skin and hair. To give your dog a healthy sheen, go over him with a hound glove or mitt as well. (3) Take care when cleansing the ears not to probe too far. Use gentle strokes with a cotton ball dampened with a dilute solution of hydrogen peroxide.

2

3

119

wouldn't get snagged by brambles and the like. And when this hearty hound came into use in other areas of Europe, its appearance was adapted to suit the new terrains.

FAVORED BY ROYALTY

The rough coated Basset Hound enjoyed a great popularity not only with certain dedicated breeders, but with members of royalty as well. Queen Alexandra, the wife of Edward VII, who ruled Great Britain after the reign of Queen Victoria, kept a kennel of rough as well as smooth Basset Hounds at her estate in Sandringham. The King and Queen were devoted to dogs, as is Britain's current monarch, Queen Elizabeth II, a great granddaughter of Edward VII. However, it is not the Basset Hound that is favored by Queen Elizabeth II, but Corgis, also another small-statured breed.

ESSENTIAL DIFFERENCES BETWEEN
THE SMOOTH AND ROUGH

Aside from the obvious difference between smooth and rough coated Basset Hounds, there are others which make for two distinct dogs of differing hunting ability in the field. The smooth hounds are in a sense, true hounds, as they have the clear bell-like voice of a true hound, and give tongue most enthusiastically; and they hunt in the true tradition of scent hounds—with their noses ever at the ground, following a trail in their sure manner.

The rough coated Basset Hound, however, hunts in a manner more befitting a terrier, as the roughs are not as steady on the trail as are the smooths, and they do not have that much-appreciated bell-like voice. As well, the roughs tend not to be as short of leg as the smooths, hence their inability to keep their noses to the ground for long periods. The roughs can, though, because of their longer legs, cover a wider range of territory in much less time than the smooths, with their extremely short crooked legs.

The rough Basset was exhibited to some extent in England during the 1800's, and a group of excellent specimens was shown at the famous Cruft's show in 1892. Those Bassets had come from France, where they enjoy more popularity than in England. Some rough Bassets did in those early days of conformation shows make it to "champion" status. One was Ch. Puritan, whelped in 1897, who finished for his title in just under one year. He was a fine representative hound, of large, sturdy bone and with an excellent coat.

The appearance of roughs at the show scene in England continued until some time after the end of World War I, after which they sort of disap-

(1) When walking with your Basset Hound on lead, urge him along gently, never pulling too hard. For him to learn to heel properly, *gentle* coaxing should do the trick, if the dog is properly rewarded when he obeys. (2) Tail-wagging signifies that the pups are happily awaiting a feeding or outing.

1

2

The Basset Hound's unique scenting powers are instinctive, and are developed fully as each dog grows to maturity. The pup in (1) shows an inclination toward scenting at an early age. (2) A tracking Basset wades through high grasses as he follows a scent. (3)A harness used on tracking dogs. (4) When travelling to a field event or show with your Basset, ensure his safety by keeping him within a wire pen in the back of your car or van. This will prevent him from being jostled around, and will keep him safely out of the driver's way.

3

4

peared in any substantial numbers and suffered a decline in popularity.

Following is a standard for the rough Basset Hound, which was drawn up at the time of the breed's showings in England, by the British Basset Hound Club. This standard, written in the early half of the century, is probably not in much use today, in its present form, if at all.

Standard of Points of the Rough Basset Hound as Adopted by the Basset Hound Club

Head: Should be large, the skull narrow but of good length, the peak well developed. The muzzle should be strong, and the jaws long and powerful. A snipy muzzle and weakness of jaw are objectionable.

Eyes: The eyes should be dark and not prominent.

Ears: The ears should be set on low, of good length, and not prominent.

Neck: Should be strong, of good length, and muscular; set on sloping shoulders.

Body: Should be massive, of good length and well ribbed up, any weakness or slackness of loin being a bad fault. The chest should be large and deep; the sternum prominent.

Forelegs: Should be short and powerful, very heavy in bone, and either nearly straight or half crooked. The elbows should lie against the sides of the chest and should not turn out.

Hindquarters: Should be powerful and muscular; the hindlegs should be rather longer than the forelegs, and well bent at the stifles.

Stern: Of moderate length and carried gaily. It should be set on high.

Coat: It is an extremely important point. It should be profuse, thick and harsh to the touch, with a dense undercoat. The coat may be wavy.

Colour: Any recognizable Hound color.

Weight: Dogs 40-45 lbs.: Bitches rather less.

General Appearance: The Rough Basset should appear a very powerful Hound for this size, and on short, strong legs. The feet should be thick, well padded and not open. Body massive and good length, without slackness of loin. The expression should be kindly and intelligent. Any unsoundness should disqualify the Hound.

Point values: Head and ears, 20; body, including hindquarters, 35; the legs and feet, 20; coat, 15. Basset character 10. Total 100.

The rough Basset Hound is not seen at all in America, despite its good reception in France and its periods of great popularity in Britain. Indeed, the AKC standard for the Basset lists as a disqualification a "distinctly long coat," illustrating quite obviously that it is the short coat that is prized by fanciers.

A pair of smooth-coated Basset pups, representing the most popular coat variety. The rough-coated, or Basset Griffon, is still somewhat popular in France, while its popularity in Britain has fallen off through the years. The rough variety of Basset was "developed" to hunt in the rugged terrain of Brittany.

The smooth coat, incidentally, should have the healthy sheen of a thoroughbred race horse, and it is fostered by the frequent use of a hound glove in grooming, as opposed to a brush.

George Krehl, who was mentioned in the first chapter as a champion of the breed in England, said this of the smooth Basset in Vero Shaw's *The Book of the Dog*, published in 1881:

> The Basset par excellence, though, is the beautiful smooth-coated tricolor of Artois, and this is the type with its rich and brilliant colouring of black, white and golden tan, its noble Bloodhound-like head so full of solemn dignity, and long velvet-soft ears, the kind and pensive eye, the heavy folds of the throat, the strange fore-limbs, the quaint and medieval appearance—this is the type, I say, that will stand first in the estimation of an intelligent dog-loving public.